the success equation

three core principles that power business improvement

Karen Carter   Marilyn Love   Fiona Wilkinson

RETHINK PRESS

First published in Great Britain in 2019
by Rethink Press (www.rethinkpress.com)

To Dr Ian Hau, without whom this book
would not have been written.

Not only did he bring the three authors together many years ago,
but his extraordinary leadership has continued to inspire them to seize opportunities
and to always search out 'the key three things'.

To Stan, thank you for your
feedback which helped to shape
the book, hope you enjoy the
finished version.

Marilyn Karen Fiona

Contents

Introduction

Do you have a business challenge?

Wondering how to kick start improvements in the way you work?

Not quite sure where to start?

If you want to make changes in your business to dramatically improve how things get done and the results you achieve, then you are reading the right book.

The Success Equation will help no matter the size of your company, your job title, the extent or nature of your challenge. You might be self-employed, the head of a global company or anywhere in between. You might work in any of the functions of your business, from IT to production. You might be a team leader, team member, project manager, consultant, change manager, process supervisor, organisational leader… Wherever you sit, whatever you want to change, the Success Equation is here to help.

We – Karen, Marilyn and Fiona – have decades of practical experience in making success happen, both as team leaders and as independent consultants. We have been in your shoes and delivered improvement across all the functions typically found in most businesses, large and small. We each have a proven track record in delivering tangible business benefit and sustainable change, and share a passion for passing on our knowledge. We have coached individuals and teams, and set up and run initiatives that have fundamentally changed the way organisations approach business challenges.

If you want to radically improve performance and sustain that performance over the long term; if you want your products or services to keep getting better and better; if you want to create an environment where people are motivated to work together to ensure success, we can show you how.

We have found the application of just three key principles will accelerate achieving your business goals:

- **Destination**
- **Engagement**
- **Iteration**

These principles have been distilled from our years of experience in addressing many different types of problems and opportunities using a wide range of techniques and approaches. We have identified and refined the best from diverse disciplines including process improvement, project management and change management to discover the vital few principles that drive success.

Experience tells us that applying these tried and trusted three principles of success, through the Success Equation, consistently makes a difference in all situations. This applies equally to small everyday challenges and large-scale organisational change. Whenever things haven't worked, we have always traced the root cause back to having skimped in the application of one of the principles.

'Any intelligent fool can make things bigger, more complex.'
E F Schumacher

You could use your time to read a whole library of books on how to improve your business, or you could just read and apply the ideas from this book and start making a difference now.

How to use this book

'A journey of a thousand miles begins with a single step.'
Lao Tzu

The aim of this book isn't just to get you thinking about the Success Equation; it is to help you start applying it to your situation. Then learning will come from your own personal experience. Hence, this is an intensely practical book packed with guidance, examples and exercises to help you begin your own Success Equation journey.

We have divided the book into two main parts. The first part provides a step-by-step guide to the three principles of the Success Equation and how they can be applied. Each step is a successive iteration that will help deepen your understanding as you progress. We will suggest some small actions that you can do immediately to get started, and build up in scope and impact.

Step 1 – getting started with the Success Equation explains the success principles and gives you some quick things you can do to apply these principles *today*.

Step 2 – applying the Success Equation to your business challenge shows you how the success principles apply to a bigger challenge using a structured methodology. We will demonstrate this by taking you through a case study to achieve a specific business goal.

Step 3 – sustaining success shows you how to use the principles to maintain and enhance your initial success.

Step 4 – why the Success Equation works invites you to reflect on everything we have covered so far and re-examines the principles at a deeper level, building on what you have learnt from previous steps.

Step 5 – looking ahead to the ultimate destination describes the long-term vision: a nurturing environment which amplifies and sustains these new ways of working. We aim to whet your appetite to go further on your journey.

As you progress through the steps, you might find that what you read challenges some of the beliefs you have built up over time and appears to be contrary to conventional wisdom. Don't take our word for it; try the Success Equation out and see how the principles work for yourself.

The second part of the book contains a wealth of materials that will support you in using the Success Equation principles. As with most things, there is a wide variety of different tools and techniques you could use, but the interesting thing is that many of them share a core set of basic approaches. Here you will find simple, quick versions of the vital few things which will enable you to tackle most situations with confidence and get results:

- **Special Topics** – a few deep-dive topics which really help in understanding the overall approach

- **Success Cycle User Guide** – detailed guidance on how to use a structured methodology for applying the success principles to a business challenge

- **The Success Report** – a worked example of the report you will deliver when you apply the success principles to a specific business goal

- **Sustaining Success User Guide** – in-depth guidance on how to use the success principles to sustain initial success

- **Tipsheets** – guidance on specific tools and techniques

- **Help, I'm Stuck** – a practical guide on what to do if you hit one of the common problem scenarios

- **Reading List** – our favourite books which have inspired and enlightened us along the way

- **The Success Cycle** – the overview diagram, for ease of reference

- **The Success Equation** – for ease of reference

This book is structured to allow you to learn at the pace that your own circumstances dictate. If you want to pause after Step 1, try out some stuff and then come back to Step 2 later, you can. Or, if you want to stop at the end of the Success Equation journey and only access the resources when you need them, you can do that too. The most important thing is for you to start on your journey and build your own bank of experience in the practical application of the Success Equation.

PART 1

The Success Equation Journey

STEP 1 – Getting Started With The Success Equation

What is the Success Equation?

The Success Equation represents our conclusion that success is the logical outcome of combining three principles: Destination, Engagement and Iteration. Put simply, this means that success depends on how effectively you define your destination, engage the relevant people, and rapidly iterate to test and develop changes. When you practise the principles together, they become synergistic and work in concert to accelerate your journey to success.

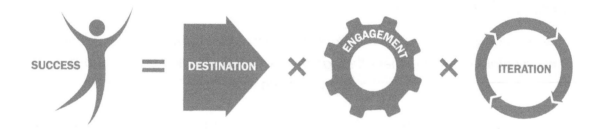

Each principle has three supporting concepts that we will outline here in Step 1 and develop further throughout the book.

What is Success?

This book isn't promising to make you internationally famous or fabulously wealthy. Our definition of success is demonstration of a significant positive change. This is not just a tick in a box where you can say that you have done something, but rather where you can show that the change has made a real difference.

Success is not achieved simply with the implementation of a new way of working; it goes further and demonstrates that the new way of working is beneficial. For example, it may be quicker or cause fewer errors. Customers and those doing the work will both feel the positive effects.

EXAMPLE

One team was successful in reducing the cycle time of their data handling processes, but felt that an equally important aspect of their success was that after they had made the changes, they were able to leave work on time. At last they were able to have dinner with their families in the evening, rather than coping with rework and backlogs.

What is Destination?

'Having an exciting destination is like setting a needle in your compass... and it will faithfully guide you there through the darkest nights and fiercest storms.'
Daniel Boone

The destination is the overall goal of your planned change. Having a well-defined destination means not only will you know when you have arrived, but also planning the route will be much easier. The more clarity you have around the overall goal of your planned change, the more successful you will be. Your destination will guide you in the right direction at every step.

There are three key concepts which will help you to define your destination:

- Start at the end
- Do what matters to your customer
- Define measurable goals

Start at the end. To define your destination, start with a succinct definition of where you want to be at the end of the change. This will enable you to work backwards to plan how you are going to get there and identify the vital few things that will be critical to success.

The more tangible the end goal is, the easier it is for you to make decisions about what needs to be done, both consciously and unconsciously. If everyone involved also understands what you want to achieve, then they can actively help you, sometimes in ways that you may not have anticipated.

EXAMPLE

At the start of a larger change, it is really powerful to mock up the report that you are going to present to your senior sponsors when you have successfully completed the change. This will help everyone to focus and engage.

Do what matters to your customer. It is vital that you describe your destination in terms that matter to those it will affect, so start by identifying your customer and seeking to truly understand their needs. Your customer is the person or group who directly receives your product or service, and may be totally different from the customer of the overall company/organisation.

Consider:

- Who is the recipient of your product or service?
- When did you last talk to them or go and see what they do?
- Do you truly know what they value about what you deliver to them?
- Do you understand what they are trying to achieve?
- What would they really value that you don't currently provide?

By focusing on what your customer needs, you can prioritise your improvement activities.

EXAMPLE

When initiating the redesign of taxi cabs, an improvement team started by observing customers using taxis. They noticed that people struggled with luggage, so they focused on improving the ease with which luggage could be moved in/out of the vehicle. The redesigned cab included a significantly larger nearside door for ease of passenger access.

Define measurable goals. A key attribute of your destination is that you can objectively assess progress.

Compare the following goal statements:

1. Improve the book delivery service
2. By 31 December, all books ordered in the UK to be delivered within forty-eight hours of orders being placed

In the first statement, there are still many unanswered questions: improve in what way, for which customers, by when…? These ambiguities slow the project down because people will make different unspoken assumptions about what it means and won't be working in alignment. Eventually the misunderstandings will surface and will need to be resolved. By then, people will be frustrated and impatient because they will rightly feel that they have been wasting their time.

You can fast-track straight past all of these distractions by making sure that you state the goal of the project in measurable terms at the start, as demonstrated in the second statement. Having measures in place, with a stated timescale, enables you to have compelling conversations with all stakeholders to gain alignment that you have correctly described the goal which reflects the primary concerns of the customer.

Measurement continues to be important once the project is ongoing as the team can then see the positive impact of their changes. Equally, with measures in place, you will know if/when things are going in the wrong direction and can investigate and adapt as necessary. Finally, at the end of the project you are equipped with an agreed objective mechanism to assess your success.

What is Engagement?

'When people are financially invested, they want a return. When people are emotionally invested, they want to contribute.'
Simon Sinek

 Just as the parts of a machine need to engage with each other and mesh together for the machine to work, the efforts of everyone involved in getting to the destination need to be engaged.

By actively engaging the attention of the participants at all stages of the project, starting at the beginning, you can build momentum for the change. This has to be a two-way process of being sincerely open, listening and taking action, rather than telling people how things are going to be. As you collectively learn together, you and your team can adjust what you are doing to propel you to success. Trust your team and those they consult. Collectively you will be far more successful than if you're making decisions on your own.

Think of engagement like the fuel in your car: without it, you can't go anywhere. If there is only a small amount, you might stutter forward briefly, but could grind to a halt at any moment. You need a decent amount to get off to a good start and will have to top up regularly to keep moving.

There are three key concepts that will help engage others to get to your destination:

- Seek to understand
- Power of the positive
- Make it real

Seek to understand. Listening to understand others' perspectives is a critical ability in engagement, as well as helping to ensure that any changes are well designed and implemented. You will need to proactively seek out what others think. Ask open questions and observe how things work in practice.

The key thing here is to adopt an open mind. Really listen. Different circumstances and drivers can profoundly affect how different individuals, or groups, view a proposed change. Understanding these underlying differences will smooth the path to success.

EXAMPLE

A team was replacing a physical gadget with an app on a smartphone. This gadget was used by many people across the company in different countries. The team saw the app as a much more convenient way of working, so were puzzled that one country's employees wanted more gadgets rather than to adopt the new app, even when the team pointed out the advantages. By talking to their customers – the employees – the team found out that only senior executives in that country used the gadget currently, and so possession was regarded as a status symbol. Once the senior executives were seen to use the app, the rest of the staff followed suit.

Power of the positive. Imagine someone comes up to talk to you about your project.

'Your project is going too slowly – what are you going to do about it?' they ask.

Someone else says, 'I think your project is really important. Help me understand how we can do it quicker.'

How do these questions make you feel? How would you respond? If you would react to the first question defensively, you wouldn't be alone. In contrast, the conversation arising from the second question would be much more productive. So if you are the person *asking* the questions, it makes sense to frame them in a way that lets the other person know that you value them and want to help.

If you were the recipient of the first question, think about how you could respond positively. Take a deep breath – the questioner obviously cares about your project. How can you harness their interest and enlist their help? Think about turning implied criticisms around to positive language and actions. It can be hard to assume that people's intentions are positive when their language is not, but doing so will smooth the path of your relationship and your project. Talk about your shared goals and how you can achieve them together.

EXAMPLE

A senior project manager was concerned that his team was hiding issues from him, worried that they would be blamed for any problem. The next time an issue came to his attention, he sent a message thanking the person for the early identification of the problem, and copied in the rest of the team asking them how they could help resolve it. Subsequently, other team members became far more forthcoming, knowing that their concerns would be dealt with in a positive way.

Make it real. Whatever you are trying to achieve, there is always much to discuss and many ideas bouncing around. If you can somehow make your ideas come alive and feel real to people, they will quickly grasp where to focus their attention and then be able to contribute more effectively.

A simple way of encouraging this is to make the team's ideas and plans easy to see and change.

EXAMPLE

A project team posted all their documentation on one wall of their team room. This was the go-to place if anyone wanted to know anything about the project. Most of the information was handwritten on flipchart paper and sticky notes. When someone needed to update the status, they just put it on the wall. If something needed discussion, the team gathered around the wall and agreed updates together.

When the sponsor reviewed the project, instead of the usual formal presentation, she reviewed the wall with the team. She too wrote on the flipcharts and added a few sticky notes. The sponsor's feedback was that, by actively contributing, she felt more involved and engaged, compared to passively reviewing updates.

Another tried-and-tested technique to make it real is to create a framework which provides a structure for discussion. This could be as simple as a mock-up of a proposal or a standard template for meetings, or something more major like a standardised methodology for running projects.

One of the best ways to bring an idea or proposal to life is to make it personal. A great starting point for a new project is to describe why you personally believe the proposed change matters and your hopes and dreams for the future, as well as more conventional objectives. You could also role model the behaviour or change that you're proposing. For example, if you are trying to persuade others to make meetings more effective, you could start by personally making sure that the aim is clear for all your agenda items *before* starting the discussion.

Throughout this book, you will find many examples of making it real to help you establish your own ways of working. By using a framework, making things visible and injecting a personal perspective, you will always smooth the path to success.

What is Iteration?

'Action is the foundational key to all success.'
Pablo Picasso

 Iteration is a rapid repeating cycle of action and learning.

Most people's natural inclination when they want to get something right is to take their time to carefully analyse, craft and perfect it before showing it to the wider world. They spend a lot of time and money on technical experts to sit at their desks, designing the 'perfect' solution. This will usually get reviewed and approved by senior managers, who may have little/no understanding of what is really needed. Unsurprisingly, a solution created in this way never lives up to expectations.

Alternatively, you could adopt an *iterative* approach and acknowledge that no one knows everything. Even a group of experts has unconscious assumptions that inform what they do. By repeatedly selecting a change that can be quickly implemented, testing it, systematically reviewing the results and identifying the changes that work, you will significantly accelerate progress towards your destination. Our philosophy is fundamentally rooted in this view of improvement as a *journey*, not a single step.

In this book, you will be learning and building your knowledge step-wise through the Success Equation journey. We can similarly describe an iterative approach to improving your business as an improvement journey.

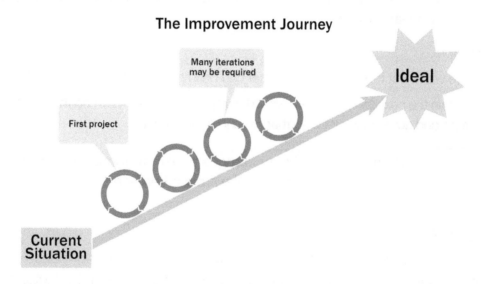

The Improvement Journey

The principle of rapid iteration is the foundation of many improvement methodologies, with Walter A Shewhart and W Edwards Deming often cited as being the founding fathers of this approach. The big advantage of rapid iteration is that it gets you to your ideal destination quickly. Additionally, you will be able to react to and take advantage of things that change as you go. Rapid iteration encourages innovation, and companies that adopt this approach stay ahead of the competition.

There are three key concepts supporting the principle of rapid iteration:

- Less is more
- Learn by doing
- Use evidence to make decisions

Less is more. The more frequently you can iterate, the better, and key to this is keeping things small. By constraining the resources involved (people, time, money, effort), you can implement quickly and find out what really works. You can then make an informed decision on what to adjust for the next iteration.

The most powerful trick to achieve this is time boxing. This is specifying a fixed date or time, and then constraining the work in order to meet the timeline – no ifs or buts. Anything that doesn't fit into the time box can wait until the next iteration, when you have learnt more.

For example:

- We will select the improvements that can be implemented within six weeks
- Within the next thirty minutes, we will complete the discussion on this agenda item and agree next steps so that we can move forward

Specifying a short timescale really encourages a team to focus their efforts on a few activities or a small scope that will make a big difference.

EXAMPLE

A sales force of about 300 reps had problems with the performance of their laptops. The technical experts suggested upgrading the laptops at huge expense and disruption to the reps' day-to-day work. Instead, a small team took copies of a representative sample of real computers and gave themselves *one week* to try out lots of different modifications to see what worked. They identified three simple things that they could implement within six weeks.

These rapid low-cost changes made a huge difference to the sales force's speed of working.

One way of applying less is more is to find the top three things that will make a difference. The power in this is *not doing* any of the other things, because they are distractions and will diffuse the effort.

Learn by doing

'Those who do not learn from history are doomed to repeat it.'
George Santayana

This saying is certainly true – we can learn a lot from things that have already happened, but the trick for truly effective learning is to *create* history – to make things happen so that we can learn from them.

By actually trying something out, we can get the evidence we need to learn.

Instead of spending a long time on exploring theoretical knowledge or getting many expert opinions to come up with a perfect design, treat improvement ideas as theories to be tested and improve your understanding of what does and doesn't work. This will quickly build and expand your team's knowledge from a much more powerful source.

Think of the amount of practice it takes to learn how to do almost anything well. You try it, look at the results, make adjustments to your technique and try again. This propels you towards better performance each time. You can consciously harness the power of repeated learning cycles, especially when you combine it with the use of evidence to make decisions.

EXAMPLE

A team in a pharmaceutical company wanted to improve reports to monitor patient enrolment in clinical trials. An IT system created the reports by combining information from many different sources. The subsequent reports were hard to understand or use.

The team used 'start at the end' by making sure they understood the decisions the report users needed to make. Then they mocked up some test reports and used these to get feedback from the users to identify what was *most* important. The team adjusted the reports accordingly and the improved reports were a huge success due to their clarity and usefulness.

Use evidence to make decisions. When you're thinking about making a change, how will you know that it has worked? What will you physically see? How will you know that the result is an improvement on what you had before?

A fundamental consideration is that decisions and actions need to be based on sound logical evidence.

In the same way that you need to know when you have reached your destination, you need to know at every stage of the change you're implementing how far you have progressed. By using evidence to assess how you are doing, you can make good decisions on what to do next.

Using evidence to test a theory allows you to make decisions on a solid basis. Getting data by measuring the results of your tests gives you the opportunity to understand if you have identified the real root causes of the problem. Then you can be confident that any improvement will be sustained and not just a one-off fluke occurrence.

You can use a wide variety of evidence to make your decisions, not just hard data. Qualitative data can, for instance, help you identify the key people to engage in your change. Start by simply looking at the data you already have, or alternatively, identify what data you can obtain quickly and easily to help you understand the situation.

EXAMPLE

An IT call centre team was trying to reduce the number of calls to the helpdesk. They were convinced that a particular system was causing the majority of the issues, so they took a month's worth of calls and grouped them into categories. To their surprise, the highest volume of calls was due to password reset requests; the system they had assumed was the major culprit actually only triggered the third biggest volume of calls.

The power of the Success Equation

Now that you are familiar with the three principles and the concepts that make up the Success Equation, do any of these principles resonate with you? Are you doing some of these things already?

Here's the big insight… the real magic happens when you apply the principles *in combination.*

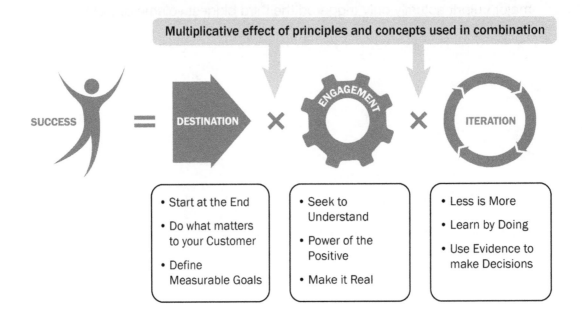

The multiplicative effect is phenomenal! It is far more impactful to apply all three principles than to do a brilliant job of one and neglect the others.

Now we have described the principles, we would like to give you a chance to try them out for yourself and start experimenting, so we have written the next section to kick start your journey by suggesting a few things to do today. Take a look, try something and reflect on it. Just doing a few small things now will really help you understand what this book is all about. Then you will be well equipped for Step 2 where we explore how to apply the Success Equation to bigger challenges.

Quick-start guide – tools and ways of working you can use today

The success principles and concepts apply not only to implementing long-term strategies, but also to small day-to-day activities and everything in between. For further details on many of the techniques, see the relevant tipsheets in Part 2.

Quick-start tool: SDP

DESTINATION   Start at the end

Each time you write a proposal or need to work out how to proceed with an issue, start by documenting your situation, destination and proposal. Defining these three elements will really help to make sure that you're clear about what you want to achieve and how you are proposing to get there.

Situation – the current issues and what impact they have.

Destination – what you want to achieve: a positive, specific and preferably measurable goal that you can achieve in different ways.

Proposal – how you are going to get from your situation to your destination. Include the actions (who, what, when) you will need to take to get there.

   Related tipsheet: SDP.

Quick-start tool: Go and see (aka Gemba)

 Do what matters to your customer

Whenever you are wondering what you should focus on, start by finding out what matters to your customer. You can do this with a simple survey or even a phone call. An even better approach is to actually go and see your customer using your product or service. We make all kinds of unspoken (and even unconscious) assumptions. It is hard to overestimate how much you can learn by visiting your customer and saying that you want to better understand what they do and how they use your product/service. Look carefully at what is going on and ask open questions to help you find out:

- What specific issues/opportunities are there in the way they are currently using your product or service?

- What challenges/issues are they dealing with – is there something you could do to help?

- What type of changes are they planning – how will you need to adapt?

During the visit, regularly reflect back what you've learnt to the people that you're talking to so that they can confirm or correct it.

The insights that you gain from such a visit will inform the decisions you make about your improvement strategy. By making this kind of trip, you also deepen your relationship with your customer by showing that you genuinely care about meeting their needs.

📄 **Related tipsheets:** Defining your customer; Paraphrasing.

Quick-start tool: What are we trying to achieve?

 Define measurable goals

When groups are making decisions, unspoken assumptions and different expectations often lead to prolonged debate. Make a habit of asking, 'What are we trying to achieve?' This will help make your destination clearer and focus the discussion.

Delve deeper by exploring:

- How will things be different when we have achieved our goal?
- What evidence will we see?
- How might we measure this?

By thinking these questions through, you will get the clarity you need to align and focus. The questions also work to focus your own thoughts when you are working through a problem alone.

EXERCISE

When you're working out what topics to raise in your next meeting with your line manager, think about what you actually want from your boss, for example 'I want Peter to show his support for our project by attending our next team meeting' rather than 'I must talk to Peter about our project'.

 Related tipsheet: Performance chart.

Quick-start tool: Paraphrasing

 Seek to understand

Ensuring everyone is aligned so that you can work together effectively is a key aspect of engagement, and this requires you to be confident that you are correctly understanding what others are saying. A really simple way of doing this is to paraphrase and summarise back what you have heard, giving them the opportunity to correct you. Make a habit of doing this after someone has made a key point. This will ensure that you stay closely aligned and avoids issues caused by misunderstandings further down the line.

Effective paraphrasing often requires summarising – a five-minute explanation won't need a paraphrasing response of the same length!

As well as alignment, the other major benefit of paraphrasing is that people feel that they have been listened to and that you are sincerely committed to understanding their perspective.

 Related tipsheet: Paraphrasing.

Quick-start tool: Spotlight success

 Power of the positive

It is tremendously powerful and energising to make a point of routinely celebrating successes along the way. This is how to do it.

Notice what *is* working/going well; if it isn't obvious, then look harder! These do not need to be big things; in fact, the message is even more powerful if they are small things because you are sending out the signal that even small actions are being noticed and appreciated.

Regularly reflect on the things that are going well with your team/colleagues. The key word here is 'regular'. For example, add a good news agenda item to the start of weekly team meetings. Make sure you credit those concerned, and mention the behaviour that helped, for example: 'From the collaborative partnership between John in IT and Kim from Sales, we have now got a system that really supports us in resolving customer complaints.'

Build on success. What can you learn; how can you repeat this elsewhere; can you use an element of what is working to help address a problem area?

EXAMPLE

One project team was under enormous pressure and morale was low. The project manager started issuing a 'Good News Update' – in the form of a weekly bulletin. Sometimes there were major events to report, other weeks there were only minor triumphs.

The impact was almost instant: tension drastically reduced and morale improved. One week the bulletin was delayed; the following day, the project manager received an email from the head of the entire division querying what had happened to the bulletin, as this was the one email he looked forward to each week.

Quick-start tool: Develop a strawman

 Make it real

When presented with a conceptual or theoretical proposal, most people build ideas in their mind, often referencing past experiences. Then when they start to share their ideas, they talk about what they see in their mind – not realising that this may be quite different from what other people are imagining. Heated debates often ensue as different people discuss different things without realising what the differences are.

Creating a strawman, ie a rough draft for comment, cuts through this painful discussion. Everyone is now looking at the same thing – the idea that was in the creator's head made real. The discussion will be much quicker and more effective as people will specify how their ideas differ from the proposal.

EXERCISE

Next time you want input on a proposal, create a strawman to illustrate what your idea will be like in practice. This can be a mocked-up report, an outline plan, a presentation, a design or almost any other artefact. If you don't have some specific elements yet, don't let that stop you – put in placeholders to be explicit about the gaps.

🎁 **Related special topic:** Increasing engagement in meetings.

Quick-start tool: Time boxing

   Less is more

It may sound trivial, but the simple act of setting a time limit for activities has a powerful effect.

Set the date. Putting the date of your project's celebration meeting in your sponsor's calendar will give your team a fixed goal to aim for and focus their efforts accordingly.

But this doesn't just apply to long-term goals – how many times have you been in a meeting where actions get assigned but without a date? And how often have those actions just drifted off into the future and never been completed, despite best intentions? Whenever you have a task or an action, assign a date for its completion.

Time box the agenda. Time wasting in meetings has to be at the top of most people's pet business hate list. Time boxing is a powerful tool that drives focus. Apply it to your meeting agenda – assign time slots for different items and rigorously enforce them. If you don't complete an item, see if there is another way to address it. Maybe the item needs discussion offline; perhaps someone could draft a situation destination proposal (SDP). Ensure the action is clearly assigned with a timeline and come back to the item at the next meeting.

Model the behaviour you want to see and ensure that agenda items are well prepared to enable them to be completed in the given timeframe. Participants will follow suit and your meetings will become more productive and efficient.

    Related tipsheets: Meeting maps; SDPs.

Quick-start Tool: AAR

 Learn by doing

Each iteration of a regular meeting is an opportunity to learn and improve, and this doesn't need to take long. At your next meeting, assign the last five-minute agenda item as an after action review (AAR). Ask each participant to quickly reflect on 'what went well' and 'what can be improved'. There are lots of different ways you can do this – for example, by going around the room asking each person to speak in turn, or putting sticky notes on a flipchart.

When everyone has contributed, agree what you will all do differently at the next meeting. Record the decision and ensure it is clear who will implement it and when.

As you iterate, your meetings will become more productive and effective. There will also be better engagement as participants will see that they can influence not only the content, but also the conduct of the meeting.

Tip: don't wait until the end of a big project to conduct your first AAR. It is far better to do AARs quickly and frequently to drive rapid improvement.

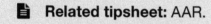 **Related tipsheet:** AAR.

Quick-start technique: Seek out data

 Use evidence to make decisions

Each time you make a decision, you are also making assumptions about, for example, the scale of the problem, the cause of the problem, the benefit of a proposal, many of which are unconscious. We believe that testing those assumptions, with evidence, will help you make better decisions.

The next time you have a decision to make, ask:

- What evidence would help me make a better decision?
- What data is available to me? The data can be quantitative or qualitative.
- Could I take a sample to help me decide?

🎁 **Related special topic:** Collecting and reporting data.

STEP 2 – Applying The Success Equation To Your Business Challenge

Where can the Success Equation be applied?

In Step 1, we introduced the basic principles of the Success Equation: Destination, Engagement and Iteration, and explored how to apply these to your day-to-day ways of working. In Step 2, we will provide a simple and robust methodology for applying these principles to larger challenges where you want to change or implement something new or different. These challenges can come in many different forms and sizes.

For example, you might want to:

- Develop a training programme

- Design a marketing campaign

- Implement new software functionality

- Increase sales

- Reduce errors in your invoicing process

- Reduce the time it takes to deliver a service

- Improve the quality of your product

- Reduce manufacturing costs

These could all be called 'projects', right? But they certainly seem like *different* projects: training, marketing, IT, sales, process improvement, productivity, product development, manufacturing… It is easy to believe that different types of projects will need fundamentally different methodologies in order to be successful, yes? In our view, **no**! We believe there is a standard methodology which can usefully be applied to all of these because they all have something in common:

After the project has been implemented, something will have 'changed'.

What may have changed?

- There is now a formal process for training where previously people just managed their own development
- There's a new marketing campaign
- An IT system has been updated
- Sales have increased
- Invoice errors have reduced
- Time to deliver a service has come down
- Product quality has improved
- Costs have been reduced

Furthermore, our expectation is always that **the change will be beneficial**. But the idea that the change will be beneficial often remains quite abstract, really just a vague notion. Indeed, people sometimes actively negate the idea that the change will be beneficial with statements like:

This isn't about making improvements; this is about saving money.	The goal needs to be described in terms of reducing costs *while maintaining current standards* of service or product. If you can reduce costs while maintaining standards, **this absolutely represents an improvement**.
This isn't an improvement; this is about setting up something completely new.	People often say this when what they really mean is, we are going to create a standard way of doing something which was previously ad hoc, eg training. It is usually fairly easy to quantify the problems of the old approach in terms of expense, time and quality. Furthermore, defining your goals in these terms will provide direction and guidance as you progress and enable you to clearly **demonstrate the benefit** of the new approach.

| This isn't really about improvements; this is just keeping up with the latest software. | Some of us love shiny new software and may have a deep appreciation of new options and clever extra functionality, based on skilled understanding of how the new tech works. Ordinary users are generally considerably less impressed. It takes time to master the new approach, which slows down the basic function of getting work done, so people rarely use all of the extra functionality, and often it is not at all clear that the disruption was worthwhile.

If a software update is optional, then gather customer input on current issues in order to decide whether to proceed, and set goals which relate to customer needs. Once more, **this represents an improvement**. |

To summarise, many projects can, and should, be articulated in terms of the benefit/improvement that you hope they will achieve. But have we convinced you yet? You may still be thinking that your situation is different.

For example, you may be considering outsourcing part of your current operation and hoping that you can just hand responsibility over to a third party without specification of the performance required and expected benefits. Take a moment to reflect on the examples above and consider if there might be a better way to proceed.

For some projects, it is obvious that you need to express goals in terms of benefits, eg increase sales; decrease delivery time etc, but for many more, it is less obvious *but equally important*. If you skip this step and fail to explicitly spell out the benefit you hope to deliver, then there is a real chance that you *won't* be successful.

For example:

- The funding for the training programme gets slashed because it is not clear that it is actually saving a lot of money while improving the core capabilities of the organisation

- The new software is reversed out because there have been so many user issues during implementation
- Customer complaints shoot up because the cost-saving initiative failed to identify the key aspects of quality which must be protected

Irrespective of the type of project, our methodology, called the Success Cycle, will support you in defining the benefits you are hoping to achieve, and then guide you in the delivery of that beneficial change.

Introduction to the Success Cycle

We have distilled the key activities into a four-stage cycle. When you have completed all four stages, you will have completed your first iteration. Long-term success may well require multiple iterations around the Success Cycle.

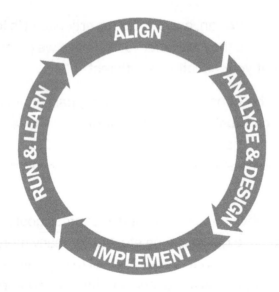

The principle of rapid iteration forms the basis of many methodologies in the areas of process improvement and change management. The Success Cycle takes inspiration from all of these, and is particularly based on our extensive experience of using the Fast Cycle improvement approach – see the Reading List for more details.

In order for your project to succeed, you need to conduct each stage of the cycle using effective engagement techniques, and be inspired by your overall destination.

We talked in general in Step 1 about what we mean by success. Now we are going to be more specific. In fact, we have templated a project document which we call the success report. This is the document you will ultimately use to demonstrate delivery of project benefits, but with the concept of 'start at the end', we actually start working on it right at the beginning of the project, using, for example, mocked-up data to illustrate target benefits.

By completing all the sections in the success report together with your team, you will ensure that all the key things get done to drive success.

SUCCESS REPORT

1. Current situation
2. Project destination
3. Project plan outline
4. Implementation details
5. Sustaining the change

The success report is a living document which you and your team will regularly update as you progress through the project. You will also use it as an engagement tool to repeatedly check that everyone is committed to, and working towards, the same goal.

There are specific milestones associated with each phase of the Success Cycle and target timelines to achieve these:

Timelines are an important part of managing the project. We have suggested standard timelines for a significant business challenge, but your challenge may be able to move considerably more quickly.

These are the golden rules for managing timelines:

- Set up your timelines at the start.

- Make sure they are short. Remember you are now embracing the concept of iteration where you repeatedly make changes and learn from them.

- Remember to allocate enough time in the Run & Learn phase to collect sufficient data to quantify the benefit your project is delivering and evaluate the effectiveness of the changes you have made. It is not a valid approach to shorten the overall timelines by cutting out this step.

- Do not change your timelines part way through. When you hit obstacles, change what you do so that it will still fit in the timeline. This will strongly boost your chances of success.

This is the first major application of the idea of time boxing and 'less is more', as we discussed in Step 1.

The four phases of the Success Cycle are:

Phase 1: Align. In this phase, we are mobilising the key stakeholders by developing their shared common understanding of the current situation, the destination and the project plan. Whatever type of project we are engaged in, it is critical to have key stakeholders, including customers, on board and aligned in their understanding and expectations.

For example, in the development of a new training programme, the current situation may be that there is no formal training; employees just manage their own development and get managers to approve events they have an interest in. Employees may be interested in how quickly they can access approved training and improve their skill levels. However, managers may be more interested in how long it will take to get the whole workforce to an agreed minimum skill level and cost.

By the end of the Align phase, the team and all stakeholders will have agreed the current situation, destination and project plan, and documented these in a draft success report.

Phase 2: Analyse & Design. While all of the principles and concepts of Destination, Engagement and Iteration apply throughout all of the phases, one concept really comes to the fore in this phase: 'use evidence to make decisions'. To be more specific, base your changes on a thorough understanding of the key factors controlling the delivery of benefit. You and your team will work through a series of structured meetings to analyse the current situation and data on current performance in order to understand the root causes of issues.

To bring a different perspective, the team can also use the 'power of the positive' and take time to understand what the ideal might look like, particularly from a customer perspective. The team evaluate potential improvements in terms of how much benefit they will contribute and how quickly they can be implemented. The team of people who really understand the situation make these decisions collectively.

By the end of the Analyse & Design phase, the team will have an agreed set of proposals and details on how and when they will be implemented. Again, you will have documented these details in an updated version of the draft success report.

Phase 3: Implement. This phase is about sticking to delivering the plan you set out at the end of Analyse & Design. The goal is to build and deliver the change within the target timeline. There will be myriad opportunities to get distracted or held up, so regular meetings are vital to keep the whole team engaged and on board.

By the end of the Implement phase, the team will have launched the change.

Phase 4: Run & Learn. This phase is so often skipped, yet is the keystone for learning. The purpose of this phase is to collect data and observe the change in operation, in order to evaluate the benefit being delivered, and to identify any further actions or adjustments which may be required. The team closely monitors how the customers are benefiting from the changes. Furthermore, the team needs to put in place plans to ensure they embed the change and sustain success in the long term.

By the end of the Run & Learn phase, which is also the end of the first iteration of the Success Cycle, the team will have delivered quantified benefits and learnt a great deal about how to deliver real and lasting change, all concisely documented in the final success report.

The role of meetings in the Success Cycle

Meetings are used throughout the project to manage overall progress:

	Align	Analyse & Design	Implement	Run & Learn
Meetings	Informal meetings to develop draft success report.	• Kick-off & Analyse. • Design. • Integration.	Team meet weekly to manage actions in implementation.	• Team meet weekly to review data and learn. • Close-out meeting.

In the Align phase, these meetings are relatively informal as you collaborate and gather input to set the destination. As the project progresses, meetings become more structured, focused on achieving predefined outputs at each stage.

How the principles fit with the Success Cycle

The following matrix illustrates, at a high level, how to use each principle within the Success Cycle when you undertake a larger improvement. It shows the key activities to perform during each phase and which principle guides each activity.

Phases of the Success Cycle:

Principles	Align	Analyse & Design	Implement	Run & Learn
DESTINATION	Draft the Success Report Ensure goal matters to your customer Define goal in measurable terms	Select improvements aligned to the measurable goal	Evaluate any changes to plan in terms of impact on goal	Evaluate results in terms of overall impact on goal and customer
ENGAGEMENT	Understand customer's problem Mockup future results Draft the Success Report *with* team and sponsor	Deepen team understanding of current situation Use positive description of ideal to inspire solutions Make proposals real using SDP format	Entire team meets regularly to review progress and manage issues	Team evaluates results together Celebrate with sponsor
ITERATION	Set short-term fixed milestones Gather evidence on problem and goal	Use evidence to analyse the problem / opportunity Identify root causes Select a small number of time-boxed improvements	Deliver solutions in fixed time, no extensions	Use data to learn what works Take actions based on data Prepare for next iteration

As you can see, all the principles are at play during all phases of the Success Cycle. It is the combined use of the principles that ensures success throughout the improvement journey. Note that the activities listed under each phase are grouped by principle only and are not necessarily shown in the order of completion.

To demonstrate how the success principles work through the Success Cycle to deliver a significant improvement, we will describe a complete worked example in the form of a case study. You can find more detail on how to apply the entire Success Cycle, from start to finish, in the Success Cycle User Guide in Part 2.

Sam's story: Applying the Success Equation through the Success Cycle

Sam is an aspiring manager working for an online retailer. Your business problem may seem quite different from Sam's, but the application of the principles and the Success Cycle will be similar for any significant business change. As you go through the case study, think about how Sam's activities could be applied in your situation.

Sam is responsible for the customer service team supporting the UK sales division, and has a small team of people who report directly to her. She sincerely wants to make a difference, but is secretly a bit worried about how to engage her team, and even more anxious about how to impress her boss, Jo, who has just given her a bit of a challenge...

Sam's story will show how the principles and concepts work out in practice through each phase of the Success Cycle, so read on to find out more.

Success Cycle Phase 1: Align

'Don't look for the solution. Look for the alignment – it will bring the solution.'
Abraham Hicks

The Align phase is the start of Sam's journey through the Success Cycle. At the end of this phase, she will have gained agreement on the first three sections of the success report:

SUCCESS REPORT

1. **Current situation** ✔
2. **Project destination** ✔
3. **Project plan outline** ✔
4. Implementation details
5. Sustaining the change

Sam identifies who has a stake in the issue and goes to find out more by talking to people and observing what happens in the process. As she engages her team and other stakeholders in crafting the first three sections of the success report, she finds that she rapidly gains alignment and momentum…

Sam also goes along to listen in to some of the calls to the customer service team to ensure she understands her customers' problems…

Together with her stakeholders, Sam uses the evidence that they have gathered to define the current situation in the success report. She states the customers' problem, and summarises how the current ways of working lead to issues and their impact on the customer:

1. Current situation

Customers' problem:

UK customers have been experiencing difficulty with deliveries. Issues related to book deliveries account for 62% of the complaints to the UK customer service team. Furthermore, these customers wait up to 10 days for complaints to be resolved, with an average of 5 days to resolution. This is reducing repeat business and potentially driving down sales.

Current process diagram, issues and impact:

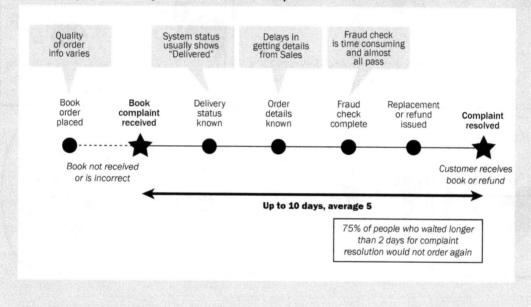

Summarising the data and discussion in this way makes it real for everyone, which in turn makes it easy for them to engage.

DESTINATION

The principle of Destination is applied through the discussion and development of a measurable goal. This enables everyone to understand exactly what the project aims to achieve.

The data that Sam's team has collected on the current problem helps to focus discussions and leads the team towards defining a measurable goal…

Sam uses the project destination section of the success report to make the goal real. She documents the current performance, the goal, and mocks up what the final results of the project will look like:

2. Project destination

Goal statement:

Reduce complaint resolution time for the northern region from a maximum of 10 days to a maximum of 2 days by 4 July.

Performance chart:

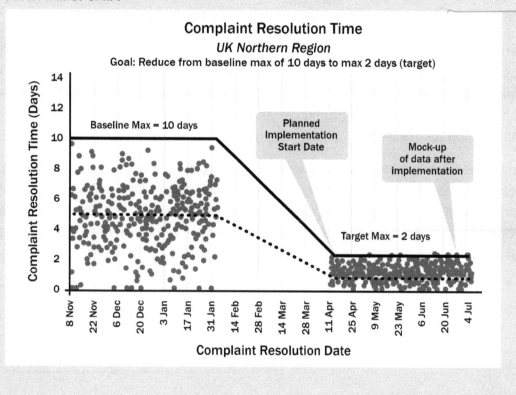

Mocking up the data to show the intended results makes the goal tangible for everyone to discuss and agree. Looking at the project destination, together with the current situation, makes it clear that the goal really matters to Sam's customers.

 Sam is rigorously applying the principle of Iteration throughout the Align phase. She and her team gather evidence, learn from it and repeatedly refine the current situation and destination, as documented in the success report. This **Iterative** approach is key to alignment on the **Destination** and overall **Engagement** in the project.

Before proceeding any further, Sam makes sure a well-defined project plan is in place. The team will rapidly take action and learn from it by agreeing short fixed milestones for each phase. Agreeing these at the start will time box the project activities, enabling the team to apply the concept of 'less is more'.

Sam's team uses the standard milestones, timelines and meetings defined in the Success Cycle User Guide – your project may be able to do it even faster. Sam makes the milestones real by fixing their dates in the project plan outline section of the success report. Adding the planned dates for team meetings also helps to sharpen the team's focus.

Now that Sam has gained alignment on the first three sections of the success report, she has completed the Align phase of the Success Cycle. She has used the principles of Destination, Engagement and Iteration to mobilise key stakeholders around a common goal with all the necessary clarity and commitment to ensure success.

3. Project plan outline

Milestones:

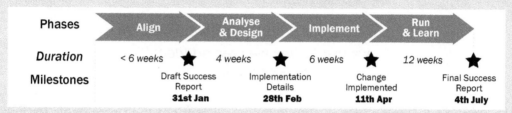

Team members:

Sponsor – Al Shah, UK head of sales and marketing
Owner – Sam Goodman, head of UK customer service team

Team members:
- Leslie Jones, UK book order specialist (supplier)
- Sarah Franklin, northern region customer service team leader (process operator)
- Stephen Andrews, UK northern area customer service team (process operator)
- Susan Goodwin, UK fraud investigator (process operator)
- Nick Wiseman, online forum moderator (customer representative)
- Ash Pitman, data analyst (support)

Meeting dates:

Event	Date
Kick-off & Analyse meeting	4 Feb – full day
Design meeting	11 Feb – full day
Integration meeting	21 Feb – full day
Weekly meetings	Every Tuesday 10–11am from 28 Feb–27 June
Close-out meeting	4 July – 9–11am
Celebration event	7 July

Success Cycle Phase 2: Analyse & Design

Align ▸ **Analyse & Design** ▸ Implement ▸ Run & Learn

*'We cannot solve our problems with the same thinking
we used when we created them.'*
Albert Einstein

In the Analyse & Design phase, Sam's team will prepare their proposals for implementation. Applying the concepts of 'use evidence to make decisions' and 'power of the positive' will ensure the proposals are based on sound logical analysis and bold enough to really make a difference.

Sam and her team have just four weeks to do this.

By the end of this phase, they will be able to further update the success report with the information to complete Section 4, the implementation details.

SUCCESS REPORT

1. Current situation
2. Project destination
3. Project plan outline
4. **Implementation details** ✔
5. Sustaining the change

This phase is highly collaborative. The team will work closely together through a series of structured meetings to deepen their understanding of the current situation and form a shared vision for the future. In this way, they will identify a set of solutions which they all support, rather than each advocating their own pet projects.

Now that Sam and the team are clear about the goal and the current situation, they will be tempted to jump into developing solutions, but it is worth spending a short amount of time identifying the root causes of the problem they're addressing.

Sam's team further analyses the current situation to identify the root causes of long complaint resolution times. They are again applying the concept of 'use evidence to make decisions'.

The team then collects further data to identify the most common reasons for non-deliveries and obtain cycle times for getting order information and fraud checks. They consolidate the results of all their analyses on to their description of the current situation.

Sam's team updates the current situation process diagram with a summary of the information they have gathered about root causes.

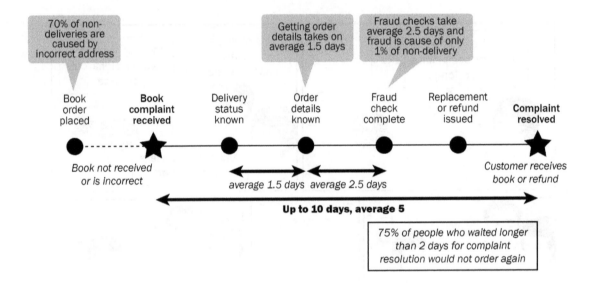

Sam and the team now have a deep understanding of what is causing long delays in getting to complaint resolution. The next step is to take a breath and think about the situation from a completely different perspective: in an ideal world, what would this process look like, particularly from the customer's perspective?

 Using the concept 'power of the positive,' Sam and her team define the ideal complaints resolution process from the perspective of the customer. This lively discussion stimulates great energy and debate.

Sam's team discussion about the ideal leads them to an insight about the complaints process...

The team then brainstorms ideas on how to move *towards* the ideal situation, based on their understanding of the root causes of the current long times for complaint resolution. Inspired by the discussion of the ideal, the team also comes up with ideas to prevent complaints happening at all. Brainstorming creates dozens of ideas and the next step is to work out which ones are the vital few that are worth pursuing.

 Sam and her team use the data and analysis they have already gathered to carefully evaluate the ideas in terms of their potential impact on their primary measure: complaint resolution time.

Additionally:

 Using the concept 'less is more' helps the team identify the small subset of improvements which they can complete by the target implementation date, 11 April.

Using this analytical approach, Sam's team quickly identifies the vital few ideas which have high impact *and* can be implemented quickly. They plot their ideas on a prioritisation matrix to help make the decisions clear.

This analysis will pay dividends when the team implements their proposals, allowing them to focus on just these few.

The team develops their selected outline ideas into detailed proposals. They are made real using the SDP format. The team specifies how they will monitor the success of the individual proposals using in-process measures. They also seek to understand how their proposals will affect those impacted and include actions to ensure effective training and communications. They consult with others outside the team to make sure that their proposals are viable. By reviewing the SDPs together as a team, they collectively agree the way forward.

They then integrate their proposals into a redesigned process and action plan. Everyone can now see how the different proposals will work together.

Implementation details from Sam's updated Success Report:

4. Implementation details

New process:

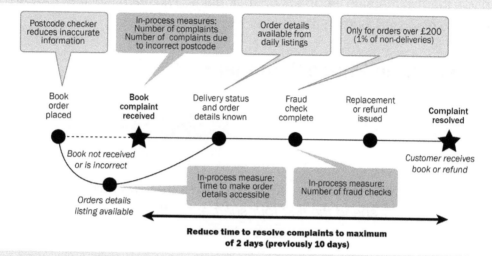

In-process measures::

In-process measures implemented

- Time to make order details accessible. Owner=Ash
- No. of complaints (overall). Owner= Sarah
- No. of complaints due to incorrect postcode. Owner= Sarah
- No. of Fraud checks. Owner= Sue

Action plan:

Change Deliverable	What	Who	By when	Done?
Access to order details	Define data extract for the order delivery details	Ash	29th March	No
Access to order details	Run a trial extract, check and adjust if necessary	IT/Ash	1st April	No
Access to order details	Start daily extracts and record time to find the details	Complaints Team	11th April	No
Limit fraud checks to orders over £200	Gain Finance approval to change	Sue	29th March	No
And so on				

Sam and her team agree the implementation details with their sponsor, Al, at their final meeting of this phase. Al is impressed with the progress that they have made and gives them immediate feedback on their plans. The team feel that they are well prepared to now start putting their plans into practice.

Success Cycle Phase 3: Implement

> '*Give me six hours to chop down a tree and I will*
> *spend the first four sharpening the axe.*'
> Abraham Lincoln

Now that the team has a well-prepared and agreed plan, the challenge during the Implement phase is to stay completely focused on executing the plan by the target date.

 Sam holds regular meetings of the entire team during the Implement phase. The purpose of these meetings is to understand whether they are on track to meet their overall goals and adjust their plan accordingly. Sam harnesses the 'power of the positive' to uncover and resolve issues and keep the team energised.

The simple integrated action plan that the team put together during the preparation for implementation is the key document they use for this. By methodically repeating the Implementation team meeting each week, they steadily progress towards the point where they can implement the change. Each meeting has the same agenda: reviewing progress, resolving issues and learning. This simple agenda enables the team to have the right conversations at the right times to ensure they remain focused on rapidly delivering the change in just six weeks.

DESTINATION

Issues will, of course, arise during implementation and these need to be acknowledged and addressed if the project is be successful. Sam ensures that the team evaluates any changes to plan in terms of impact on goal. This discussion starts with a focused question:

Are there any new issues which might impact our plan?

ITERATION

When issues arise that will impact the plan, it can be tempting to delay the project and increase the scope. Sam makes sure the team sticks to the concept 'less is more' to ensure they deliver the solutions in the fixed time, with no extras.

For Sam's team, the completion of the Implement phase means that they have successfully implemented their three key ideas to achieve their goal. And they have done this by the agreed date for the milestone of 'Change Implemented'. It has taken a huge amount of self-discipline to keep it all time-boxed and focused on the destination, and Sam's team found the meetings invaluable to ensure that everyone remained aligned.

With all their actions complete, Sam and her team launch their new ways of working and move into the final phase: Run & Learn.

Success Cycle Phase 4: Run & Learn

Align › Analyse & Design › Implement › **Run & Learn**

'Any fool can know. The point is to understand.'
Albert Einstein

This final phase is a vital learning opportunity for the team. The customers will start to benefit immediately from the changes that work, but the challenge is to collect data and feedback to objectively evaluate the impact of the changes, and to identify and resolve any issues. Finally, the team creates the plan to sustain their change.

By the end of this phase, the team will be able to complete the success report and celebrate what they have achieved.

SUCCESS REPORT

1. Current situation
2. Project destination
3. Project plan outline
4. Implementation details
5. **Sustaining the change ✔**

Weekly team meetings continue throughout the Run & Learn phase.

Unlike many teams that disband once they have implemented their solutions, Sam's team continues to meet regularly through this phase. The meetings focus on evaluating their progress and taking action, as needed, to ensure they remain on track for success. They also meet at the end of the phase to collectively agree how to sustain what they have achieved and to celebrate.

In the early days of running the new process, the team meetings focus on reviewing the in-process measures. The team has specifically set these measures up to monitor the new process and provide alerts if key steps are not running as planned.

 Sam's team applies the concepts of 'learn by doing' and 'use evidence to make decisions' during this phase. They use the in-process measure data to understand how the new process is performing and take action, as needed, to stay on track.

 As the Run & Learn phase comes to a close, Sam's team assesses the data on their measurable goal to evaluate their progress towards the destination.

The team updates the data in the chart they mocked up at the beginning of the project. By the end of this phase, they can show that the complaint resolution time has fallen dramatically from a maximum of 10 days to just 1.7 days – they have beaten their target of 2 days! They have also significantly reduced the overall number of complaints.

Performance chart for Sam's project:

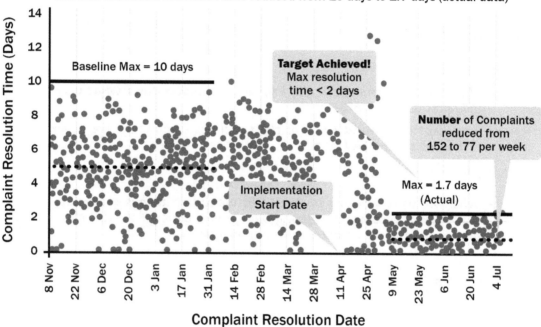

The success report is updated to show the real data, rather than the mock-up that was created during the Align phase.

At the end of the Run & Learn phase, Sam and her team create the plan to sustain the change. They work with the sponsor to identify the long-term owner and review what they have learnt from the entire Success Cycle, agreeing some actions to publicise their success and the team learnings so that this project creates ripples into the wider organisation. The team even considers what the goal might be for the next iteration of improvement.

The final section in the success report is updated with the details for sustaining success.

Here is the final section of the success report for Sam's project:

5. Sustaining the change

Process owner:

Sarah Franklin, northern region customer service team leader

Learnings (extract):

What went well?

- The root cause analysis really helped us to understand what was going on with the process
- Sam kept on reminding us of the timelines — it meant we never lost focus on the end date

What could be improved?

- When we were working on the SDPs we didn't always get input from our departments. Getting buy-in was easier if we did this and we had more confidence in our proposals.

Actions (extract):

Who?	What?	When?
Sarah	Meet with southern region customer service team to share our learnings and kick start next project	18 July
Sam	Work with southern region team and sponsor to ensure future projects use team contracts to establish team member responsibilities for getting input	31 Aug
Sam	Deliver presentation at next sales meeting to showcase our improvement and how we achieved it	5 July
Ash	Meet with IT to explore direct access to order details	31 July

You can find the full and final success report for Sam's project in Part 2 of this book.

And finally, Sam and the team celebrate their success. Sam's manager Jo, who set her the challenge, and the team's sponsor, Al, are there to congratulate them.

Reflection on applying the Success Cycle to a significant change

We have followed Sam as she used the Success Cycle to guide her through her first complete iteration and achieve a significant improvement. Here is a summary of the key elements of the Success Cycle that she followed to apply the Success Equation principles and concepts to her challenge:

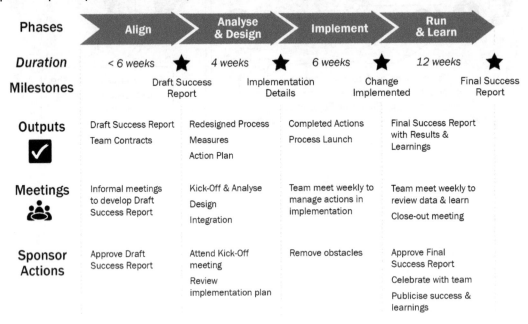

Phases	Align	Analyse & Design	Implement	Run & Learn
Duration	< 6 weeks	4 weeks	6 weeks	12 weeks
Milestones	Draft Success Report	Implementation Details	Change Implemented	Final Success Report
Outputs ✓	Draft Success Report Team Contracts	Redesigned Process Measures Action Plan	Completed Actions Process Launch	Final Success Report with Results & Learnings
Meetings	Informal meetings to develop Draft Success Report	Kick-Off & Analyse Design Integration	Team meet weekly to manage actions in implementation	Team meet weekly to review data & learn Close-out meeting
Sponsor Actions	Approve Draft Success Report	Attend Kick-Off meeting Review implementation plan	Remove obstacles	Approve Final Success Report Celebrate with team Publicise success & learnings

It was these steps that guided Sam and her team in their application of the Success Equation, so now let's take a moment to think about a business challenge that you are facing. Can you see how you might use the Success Cycle and the Success Equation principles to meet your challenge?

Of course, not all challenges are the same – and sometimes people struggle to see how this methodology will work for them. Even without meticulously following the Success Cycle, you can still use the Success Equation principles to provide a guiding light to ensure that you do the things essential to achieving success.

Here are some examples of where teams have adapted this approach to their situation:

EXAMPLE: A CORPORATE DECISION HAS ALREADY BEEN MADE

A small team was told by company executives to implement a programme that, for legal reasons, would radically change the way everyone in the company used email.

The team members engaged with the executive legal sponsor to define the goal of the change and communicate it widely. They looked at different ways of designing the details of the change, evaluated them and tried them out on a small scale, before implementing the change across the company. The implementation was successful, and disruption was minimal.

Although the employees hadn't welcomed the change, they accepted it and feedback was positive. This was in stark contrast to a previous attempt to implement a similar change, which subsequently had to be abandoned.

The team followed the Success Equation and ensured that they completed all of the key elements of the Success Cycle, even though the overall solution had already been decided.

EXAMPLE: NEW PROCESS – NO OBVIOUS BASELINE FOR COMPARISON

A team was set up to create and implement a standard way of requesting a service. Everyone agreed that this was needed because no one seemed to know who to ask or how to access the service. The team defined the goal in terms of time to action a service request, interviewing past users of the service to patch together at least some ad hoc data on how long it had taken to action a request previously.

Even though there was no established way of making the requests, the team overcame this obstacle and was able to gather enough informal data to provide a rough baseline and define a measurable goal. It was then easy to apply the Success Equation through the Success Cycle and meet their improvement target.

EXAMPLE: TEAM SET A HUGE GOAL AND LONG TIMELINES

A project team was given the goal to update a library of reusable marketing materials. Using conventional approaches, they estimated that it would take over two years to complete.

Instead, the team worked with the customers to agree a goal of increasing the use of the materials, which would in turn speed up the creation of new campaigns. They put together a small team of experienced marketeers who were quickly able to agree the top four most useful items. The team rapidly prototyped new designs for these four, and the refined designs were then produced and adopted across the marketing department.

Building on their success, the team identified the next four most useful items and again quickly got these into use. Within six months, the twenty-six most commonly used items had been redesigned, leading to a significant reduction in campaign creation time.

By redefining the goal and iterating towards it, the team was able to use the Success Equation principles not only to meet their challenge, but also to reduce the amount of work it required.

In all of these examples, the teams focused on what really mattered to the customer, applied the Success Equation principles, and adapted the steps of the Success Cycle to ensure they completed the key activities.

Many, if not most teams will be able to follow the standard Success Cycle methodology, but if you are struggling – let the principles be your guide. You can also check out the section 'Help, I'm Stuck' in Part 2 to review the common concerns raised while we have been coaching teams in the use of the Success Cycle.

Reflection on applying the Success Equation in Sam's case study

We have reflected specifically on how to apply the Success Cycle to a business goal. Let's now reflect more broadly on how Sam applied the Success Equation principles and concepts, both individually and in combination, to her significant business change.

Sam's team applied each of the success principles individually throughout their project:

They defined a clear Destination by starting at the end and defining a measurable goal that mattered to their customer. This was made real in the form of the success report and was the key focus of all their work and meetings throughout the project.

Sam focused on Engagement by seeking to understand the customer needs, the sponsor's perspective and the team's viewpoints. She used the power of the positive to keep the motivation going and turn discussion on the issues into problem-solving. Throughout the project, frameworks made it real for everyone involved, which allowed them to contribute in a dynamic and focused way.

The team achieved more with less by keeping the resources and timescales tight, consciously reflecting on learning throughout the project and using evidence to inform their decisions. This meant they could design and implement solutions in a short space of time during the first rapid Iteration of improvement.

But the principles were even more powerful when applied in combination – for example:

- In the Align phase, Sam used the mocked-up chart of her measure of success to define her **destination**. This not only helped her to set a clear direction for the team, it defined the first **iteration** in terms of time and scope as well as making it easy to **engage** her team, customers and sponsors by making it real.

- In the Analyse & Design phase, Sam's team used **evidence** to define the root cause of why complaints took so long to resolve. They evaluated potential solution ideas in terms of their impact on the **measure of success** and the **fixed milestone** for implementation. This evidence-based approach helped the team to work together to come to a **common understanding and agreement** on the way ahead.

- In the Implement phase, the team took time to understand how issues might affect their ability to achieve the first **iteration** on schedule. This consistent focus on their **destination** helped the team to **positively** address all issues.

- In the Run & Learn Phase, the team used the **evidence** they gathered from measures to help them understand how they were progressing towards their **goal** and to **inform others** about their achievements.

The combined use of the principles and concepts is where the real magic happens, as this is when you will feel the full force of the Success Equation. It is a special feeling, almost as if the project has grown wings and taken flight in terms of the enhanced momentum. There is a sense of urgency and commitment that comes from being aligned on a destination as the team realises that they have everything they need (knowledge, authority and support) to rapidly define and implement the new way forward.

Once the team members hit their stride, work stops feeling like work. People attend meetings enthusiastically as they see that this way of working is highly productive. Participation in the project becomes genuinely rewarding, even fun, as people feel appreciated and can see how their contribution is directly leading to a better tomorrow.

If you are keen to get started in applying the Success Cycle methodology to your own business challenge, there is detailed guidance in the Success Cycle User Guide in Part 2. We are now going to continue Sam's story and see what she and her team do next to make sure that their success sticks.

STEP 3 – Sustaining Success

Making the change stick

> *'We are what we repeatedly do. Excellence, then, is not an act, but a habit.'*
> Will Durant

By the end of Step 2, we had explored how the success principles can be applied to a larger challenge, resulting in a significant business improvement. Now, in Step 3, we are going to look at how the same principles can be applied to maintain and enhance that initial success.

Success requires a high level of commitment to be sustained – how many projects have you seen where, after a big fanfare, everyone goes back to their day job and nothing really changes? To ensure that success actually sticks and improvement carries on, you must continue to apply the success principles.

The good news is that this builds on a lot of the things that we have described already in the Success Cycle.

The key ways that we apply the success principles to make success stick are:

Principles	Making success stick
DESTINATION	Ongoing review and agreement on measurable goals with senior stakeholders and customers
ENGAGEMENT	Regular reviews of performance with customers and team, conducted by process owner Use a dashboard to make it real
ITERATION	Use in-process measures to monitor performance and take corrective action Identify a small number of improvements to move closer to the ideal (further draft success reports)

Let's look more closely at how to apply the principles to make success stick by following what happens in our case study. Sam and her team want to ensure that success sticks in the customer complaint process.

Sarah is the new process owner – her selection was confirmed in Section 5 of the success report, Sustaining the change. Sam, as the project leader, was responsible for delivering the improvement, which saw time to resolve complaints reduced to a maximum of 1.7 days; Sarah, as process owner, is responsible for ensuring this success sticks and that the time to resolve complaints stays low.

 Sarah sets up regular meetings with the team and with her senior stakeholders, Sam, Al and Jo, in order to review how well the complaint resolution process is working. She uses a dashboard to facilitate the discussions and make the ongoing review of the process real for everyone.

The aim of the meetings is to understand how the complaints resolution process is performing and to ensure everyone continues to focus on progress towards goals. Holding the meetings sends out a strong message: this process is important, so we will make sure it is performing as we expect. This gives the process, Sarah and her team status in the organisation.

Sarah learnt from the Run & Learn Phase in Sam's project that visible tracking of measures really helps to inform team discussion and decisions. She now makes it real for the team by using the dashboard as the basis for the meetings. For each of the measures that the team will continue to monitor, she confirms who will manage the data collection and lead the review of the latest data during the meetings. In most cases it is the same person who was responsible for the measure during the original project, but Sarah transfers responsibility for order information to one of her reports, Gill, and takes on responsibility for collecting and reviewing customer feedback herself.

Part of Sarah's dashboard:

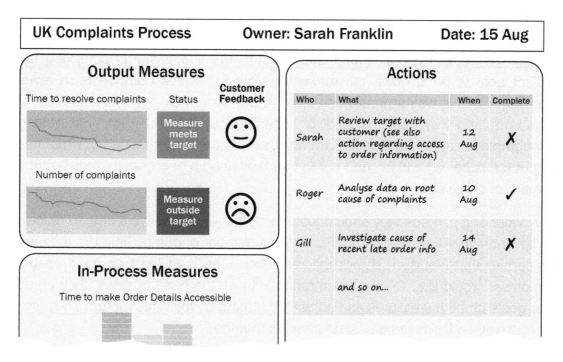

As well as the quantitative measures, Sarah also displays qualitative information from the customer feedback on how well they feel the process is performing. Sometimes there will be a difference between how the customer feels and the data (as in the display above). Discussion on this mismatch is often a fruitful source of insight. In this particular case, the team decides to feed this observation into their dialogue on goals with their senior stakeholders.

📄 **Related tipsheet:** Dashboard.

Making a change stick requires attention, determination and, above all else, persistence. The critical success factor for Sarah and her team is maintaining a *regular* review of *relevant* data.

 Sarah works with Sam, Jo and Al to agree new measurable goals for the UK complaints process for the next six months.

You will no doubt remember that Sam's team was successful in achieving the project goal to bring down the maximum time to resolve complaints to fewer than 2 days. This was a great achievement, but even their new maximum of 1.7 days is quite a way from the ideal of instantaneous resolution and not getting any complaints at all. Sarah and Sam discuss with Jo, Sam's manager, what their output measures should be, and agree that they need a new goal to decrease the number of complaints.

They wonder if perhaps they should just maintain the current cycle time to resolve complaints while focusing on decreasing the number of complaints, but they are concerned that feedback shows the resolution time is still not as good as the customers would like. Talking this through with Al, the head of sales, they agree new goals for both measures and adjust the targets on their dashboard. They also agree to review these targets again after six months.

The data from the dashboard helps Sarah's team make decisions about what actions to take and where to focus. As well as their ongoing improvements, the team identifies two further projects and will use the Success Cycle methodology to help them achieve their goals.

In the regular team meetings the team focus on review of the dashboard. Each measure has an updated entry on the dashboard with a summary of performance and whether or not it is on target. This makes it quick and easy to identify where Sarah and her team need to focus their discussions and where they need to take action. In this way, they can ensure ongoing improvement and continue to move towards their goals.

At a meeting with Al, the team also agrees the next set of projects. Together with the improvements they've identified and actioned in the review meetings, these are the next iterations on the improvement journey towards the long-term destination.

The Improvement Journey

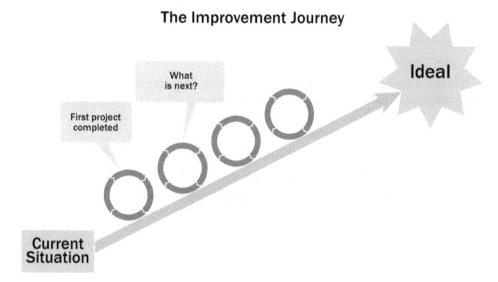

Only the northern region of the UK was included in Sam's original project. The first of the new projects extends the scope to an additional region. With agreement from Al, Jo and Sam, Sarah works with Bob, the team leader of the southern region, to implement the new complaints process there.

New project: Implement new complaints process in southern region

Owner: Bob

Goal statement: To decrease time to resolve UK book delivery complaints in the southern region from a current maximum of 10 days to a maximum of 2 days by 5 December.

In the Analyse & Design phase of the project, rather than defining root causes and solutions from scratch, the new team focuses on confirming the problem, verifying it with local data. They establish why and how the solutions that worked in the northern region will also work in the southern region.

The second new project focuses on the new goal of reducing the number of complaints and is based on the team's recent analysis of the current process.

New project: Reduce number of complaints

Owner: Sarah

Goal statement: Decrease the number of UK delivery complaints from a current average of 77 / week to 20 / week by 30 October.

The results of both of these projects and the ongoing day-to-day improvements can clearly be seen on the dashboard, as Sam finds out when Sarah invites her along to one of her regular review meetings six months later...

For more information, see Part 2: Sustaining Success User Guide.

Sticking with the Success Equation

Making your success stick requires a shift in your thinking from 'doing a one-off project' to actively managing your ongoing *process* through application of the Success Equation principles. The principles continue to work *together* to sustain the improvements that you achieved in your initial change. Success builds on success, so each iteration will be easier than the last.

As before:

- Setting and updating measurable goals aligns actions and enables engagement for new iterations of improvement
- Regular team reviews of evidence enable learning and positive action leading to success

We have described what you need to do to make success stick – but you may be questioning if you really need to do this. Maybe you believe you have a committed owner and a team who won't let things slide. They have put a lot of work into getting where they are, so surely that's enough?

You are right, that does go a long way, especially in the short term, but it is not sufficient to ensure that the gains you have made will be maintained, as the following story illustrates.

EXAMPLE

Even well-embedded changes come unstuck without the continued application of the success principles. A multi-disciplinary team was set up to improve the process for creating one of the key deliverables on the critical path for submission of new pharmaceutical products: the clinical study report. When the team started, the average time between the study finishing and the report being written was 27 weeks. After the initial improvement project, this came down to fewer than 3 weeks. Repeated iterations of improvement over the next few years brought that down even further to just 3 days.

As time went on, the original improvement team members moved on and were replaced, but the measurement and review systems meant that the new team maintained the performance, even through a period of great change as the company merged with another of similar size. Then a new leader decided that the company's strategic focus needed to be elsewhere. Without any Destination for this process, it was hard to get Engagement to carry out any further iterations of improvement, and ongoing review and management of the process ceased. The clinical study reporting time increased and quickly reverted back to the original level of 27 weeks.

The moral of this story is that even when a change seems well embedded over many years, if you stop applying the success principles, the change won't be maintained. Sometimes this is the right thing to do as circumstances change, but make no mistake, without continued application of the principles, your success will soon come unstuck.

Stick with the Success Equation and the stream of successes will continue to flow.

STEP 4 – Why The Success Equation Works

Introduction

We have already covered a lot of ground. Let's take time to reflect on what we have discussed, starting with a recap on the Success Equation:

By now, we hope this is starting to look familiar, logical and even fairly straightforward.

Success really does come from this simple approach of being clear on what you want to achieve, actively involving the relevant people, and then rapidly testing out potential improvements. The hard part is sticking to this and not getting distracted.

We looked at a structured approach to addressing specific problems or opportunities using the principles of the Success Equation. Then we moved on to explore how to sustain success and ensure that improvements keep coming. Have you tried a few things out for yourself? Hopefully you have and are getting a feel for how the principles work and are mutually reinforcing:

- The clearer you can be about the **Destination**, the easier it is to **Engage** others and identify potential improvements

- The more you **Engage** people, the more input you get to help shape the **Destination** and the faster you will be able to implement ideas

- The faster you **Iterate** through each improvement cycle, the faster everyone gains the learning which increases **Engagement** and builds momentum to propel you towards your **Destination**

In Step 4, we are going to delve deeper into each principle and the supporting concepts and consider how they can be applied. We will examine some common myths along the way and give you optional exercises to complete. When the going gets tough, this step is your resource bank to inspire and support you.

Let's get started with the principle of Destination…

Why Destination matters

'Few, if any, forces in human affairs are as powerful as shared vision.'
Peter Senge

The purpose of defining a destination is to provide direction to inform and align activities in pursuit of a common goal.

It is *not* a vague statement of aspiration. **Destination *is*:**

A succinct and verifiable description of the future, which will benefit your customers.

The principle of Destination can be applied to many different levels and timescales. While our main definition is about the change you are working on, we also use it for thinking about meetings, about the next phase of the change cycle – indeed, for starting anything. By having a clear, shared view of what you want to achieve at any point in time, you can get everyone aligned and on track.

Clarity on the destination provides a constant source of guidance on where to focus, as you can assess each suggestion, potential idea or issue by repeatedly asking:

How might this affect progress towards our destination?

Once everyone has agreed the destination, people around you feel empowered to take action.

There are so many things competing for our attention, it can be hard to choose where to focus. When we make a goal clear, it becomes much easier for people to see why they should take action, and what action to take. Then they can act with confidence because they can make their own assessment of how much their actions will help to achieve the goal.

Indeed, when people buy in to a goal, they feel compelled to contribute and sometimes help in ways that you may never have even imagined. The better people understand the destination, the more they will act spontaneously while remaining aligned by a shared vision.

Destination needs to be defined in terms of both a short-term goal for each improvement iteration *and* a long-term overall vision (or ideal state).

'Success is a journey, goals are but navigation points.'
Unknown

During the Align phase, Sam's team created a detailed specific goal as part of the draft success report.

EXAMPLE: SHORT-TERM GOAL FOR SAM'S PROJECT

Reduce complaint resolution time for the northern region from a maximum of 10 days to a maximum of 2 days by 4 July.

In the Design meeting, they also looked at the long-term vision (the ideal for the customer):

EXAMPLE: LONG-TERM VISION FOR SAM'S PROJECT

No complaints. If a complaint is received, it is resolved immediately (zero time).

Thinking about the true ideal from the customer's perspective was revealing for Sam's team. This discussion highlighted that the team needed to do much more than simply speed up complaint resolution; to really satisfy the customer, they needed to work towards eliminating the cause of complaints. This represented a complete shift in thinking, which can lead to generation of *very* different improvement ideas. In the case of Sam's team, this shift in thinking helped them to come up with solutions like the postcode checker.

Note that there is no expectation that you can instantly achieve the ideal. Indeed, it may take years of iterative improvements, but once you're clear on the true customer ideal, every improvement you make should move you in the right direction and enhance the value you offer to the customer.

Remember, you can also apply the principle of Destination to small or short-term tasks, such as your next meeting. In this context, the destination is the set of meeting outputs you want to achieve. By getting upfront agreement to a specific set of meeting outputs, you can ensure that every aspect of the meeting works towards them. The key thing is to ensure that everyone is aligned in the view that the purpose of the meeting is to deliver these tangible outputs within the timescales specified in the agenda.

EXAMPLE: KICK-OFF & ANALYSE MEETING FOR SAM'S PROJECT

Meeting outputs:
- *Agreed project destination, milestones, current situation*
- *Potential root causes*

 Related tipsheet: Meeting Maps.

When you're defining your **Destination**, there are three underlying concepts:

1. Start at the end

2. Do what matters to your customer

3. Define measurable goals

Let's review these individually.

Start at the end

> *'If you don't know where you are going, you might wind up someplace else.'*
> Yogi Berra

The purpose of starting with agreement on the end point is to ensure everyone has the same definition of success. Then you can select and plan actions to optimise the route.

By focusing on the end rather than the beginning of the journey, you are providing the impetus and the direction to start it. Ask the team, 'What are we trying to achieve?'

It is a common mistake to assume that everyone shares the same ideas about goals and vision, so you may feel it's unnecessary to talk about these. Yet even a short discussion about the destination may reveal a great range of different perspectives. Having these conversations at the start of a piece of work will ensure alignment and engagement.

Starting at the end enables you to be efficient. With a specific destination to refer to, people can discuss and agree what action they can take to contribute. Without this, the team can waste a lot of time working on unimportant things.

Every time Sam's team started a new phase of the improvement cycle or held a meeting, they started by defining the required outputs. When these were clear and agreed, they could then work backwards and define the processes and inputs they needed to get them to those outputs.

MYTH

'Spending time defining the target outcome will slow me down; I just need to get started.'

REALITY

Teams who don't have a clear destination may never get the project off the ground. Even if they do, they are likely to get stuck in analysis, unable to confidently make decisions.

EXAMPLE

One team believed that the complexity of the interfaces between a set of IT systems was a problem and should be replaced with a single IT system. Without consulting their customers, they spent eighteen months creating diagrams describing the current configuration. By the time they had finished, some parts of what they had described were already out of date. Their project never got off the ground, and when their leader moved on to another position, it was quietly dropped.

The success report is a perfect example of 'start at the end' and we make reference to it throughout the book. At the beginning of the project, Sam's success report not only contained a clear measurable goal, but also physically demonstrated the gaps which needed to be filled by the team.

Example: completion of Sam's success report elements at different phases			
Success report element:	**Align**	**Improvement phase: Analyse & Design**	**Run & Learn**
1. Current situation	✓	✓	✓
2. Project destination	✓	✓	✓
3. Project plan outline	✓	✓	✓
4. Implementation details	O	✓	✓
5. Sustaining success	O	O	✓

This is a useful technique not only for the success report, but also at other stages of the improvement process – for example, mocking up a 'strawman' design for comment enables it to be rapidly developed and completed.

You can use this technique to help you in many different situations – try the exercise below, or think of another situation where you may be able to apply it.

EXERCISE

• Think about a report or presentation that you need to create. Start by working out what you want the presentation to achieve, for example, there might be specific actions you want people to take. Create presentation headings to reflect the basic elements which need to be included to achieve your desired outcome. Add all the content that you already have. Then work on collating the missing information.

• Reflect on the difference between this and how you have previously approached presentations.

The process of defining the end is not the work of an instant. As we saw in the IT systems example above, it is something that requires discussion and engagement with others. The true power of defining a destination lies in its ability to align people's thoughts and actions. Your role as a leader is to enable those discussions to occur and bring people back to this focus when needed. 'Starting at the end' is a simple, reliable technique which will inform all subsequent activities.

Do what matters to your customer

'There is only one boss. The customer. And he can fire everybody in the company from the chairman on down, simply by spending his money somewhere else.'
Sam Walton

The purpose of doing what matters to your customer is to make sure that your destination is valuable to your organisation.

We have already touched on the importance of doing what your customer needs, and this is at the heart of defining your end goal. Think about the reason that your department or organisation exists: it is to produce or do something that someone else – your customer – needs. Your success is determined by your ability to meet their needs.

For example, Sam's success report clearly states the customers' problem and its impact.

Customers' problem for Sam's project

UK customers have been experiencing difficulty with deliveries. Issues related to book deliveries account for 62% of the complaints to the UK customer service team. Furthermore, these customers wait up to 10 days for complaints to be resolved, with an average of 5 days to resolution. This is reducing repeat business and potentially driving down sales.

Once you have started a dialogue with your customer to help understand their needs and define your goal, don't stop! You will need their continued engagement to make sure the change you design will really help them meet their goals.

📄 **Related tipsheet:** Defining your customer.

The more relevant the destination is to your customer, the easier it will be to get support and input. If the destination matters to your customer, they will be willing to spend time and energy supporting the project, and others in your company will see the benefit in improving this aspect of the service or product.

For example, Sam made sure the goal reflected customer concerns and she received strong support from the project sponsor, Al, because he could see the direct impact on sales. When the project team hit a technical problem with the order reports not working properly, Al quickly helped ensure they got the IT resource they needed.

Every step of the journey will be easier if the destination really matters to your customer:

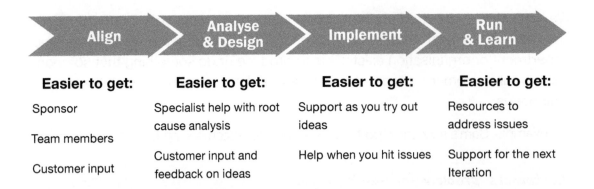

Align	Analyse & Design	Implement	Run & Learn
Easier to get:	**Easier to get:**	**Easier to get:**	**Easier to get:**
Sponsor	Specialist help with root cause analysis	Support as you try out ideas	Resources to address issues
Team members			
Customer input	Customer input and feedback on ideas	Help when you hit issues	Support for the next Iteration

In initial conversations with customers, it is helpful to use open questions to explore what is happening currently. For example, you might ask a customer:

- How do you use our product currently?
- What type of problems do you experience?
- What sort of improvements would you like to see?

Simply listening to your customer will not always give you the full picture as they may not be able to articulate what is important to them; you also need to collect data and observe the process in action to ensure that you understand their needs. Think back to the redesigned taxi door example we mentioned in Step 1. Customers hadn't mentioned struggling to get their luggage into the taxi as a problem; they expected that to happen. It was only through observation that the taxi designers discovered this as a potential opportunity for improvement.

In some circumstances, it can be difficult to make contact directly with your customer, for example because there are too many of them, or only a particular department is allowed to make direct contact. Perhaps you could contact a representative sample or talk to the people who do deal directly with the customer to understand their perspective; they may be able to carry out a structured interview for you. Even better, ask if you can shadow someone who talks to the customer directly, for example spend a day on the road with a salesman. Remember how Sam listened in to the calls to the customer complaints team in order to better understand what was happening from the perspective of both the customer and the team?

Continue dialogue with your customer throughout your project to check that their needs haven't changed and your proposed solutions really make a difference. Ideally, have a customer on your improvement team so they can keep the team focused on the destination, but failing that, check with your customer that you are on the right track during the project. The customer may not be the same in all instances – for example, you may need to try out a new website design on customers who will use it, then test out your communications on a different set.

Once you've delivered something that your customer values, you may need to re-evaluate how you define success going forward. In the past, customers were thrilled when car manufacturers provided a radio; now, people want the ability to stream music from their mobile phone.

EXERCISE

Think about a piece of work you have been asked to complete. Start by ensuring that you have defined the customer of the work. Go and talk to the customer about their relevant experiences and ask them to describe the characteristics of a good outcome from their perspective.

Define measurable goals

'If you can't measure it, you can't improve it.'
Peter Drucker

The purpose of defining measurable goals is to sharpen the clarity of what you want to achieve and enable objective assessment of progress. Translating a goal into a measurable entity is the most effective way to be really clear about it.

Ask the team, 'How will we know when we get there?'

Having a measurable goal means that when you have completed each cycle of iteration, you can demonstrate the level of benefit that you have delivered. It is also useful during the project when you're considering different potential solutions, as you can evaluate the likely impact of each and then select the solution accordingly.

Your goal needs a timescale. Keep the timescale relatively short and visible on the horizon. If the timescale is too far out, people can become complacent. Giving people a short timescale really helps to focus the mind and often produces the best work.

Setting a measurable target may seem challenging and somewhat arbitrary, but the key thing is to ensure this is aligned to customer needs. We often find that teams are amazed by what they achieve when they're set a clear, measurable goal.

With Sam's project, the team initially felt a bit daunted by the scale of their goal, but this inspired them to consider more radical ideas than they might otherwise have suggested.

EXAMPLE: GOAL FOR SAM'S PROJECT

Reduce complaint resolution time for the northern region from a maximum of 10 days to a maximum of 2 days by 4 July.

EXERCISE

Think about a piece of work that you are currently working on. How will you know if it has been successful? Ensure you have expressed the goal in measurable terms with a target date.

At the outset of your project, trying to define your primary measure can be quite confusing. Cycle time is often a good starting point: this is the total elapsed time for an activity to occur.

📄 **Related special topic:** Using cycle time as a measure.

'Teams that don't keep score are only practicing.'
Tom Malone

Measures enable us to evaluate progress objectively. Throughout the project, there should be two repeating questions beating out a background rhythm, forming a soundtrack to all activities.

Ask the team, 'How are we doing? How do we know?'

The answers come from using measures to continuously monitor performance.

It is vital that you review hard data on current performance regularly (at least weekly) to keep a razor-like focus on what is really happening. This includes the in-process measures which provide instream feedback on how well you are complying with the intended new process.

In Sam's project, the output measure was complaint resolution time. By continuously monitoring this and the in-process measures, the team was able to answer vital questions about performance at each stage of the project:

Align	Analyse & Design	Implement	Run & Learn
What is the current level of performance?	How much would different solutions improve performance?	How can we monitor key aspects of the new process?	Are there any unexpected issues with the new process?
			How much has overall performance improved?

REALITY

Everyone likes to think that the result of their efforts will be abundantly clear. The reality is that without a well-defined measure, people will come up with their own ways of assessing your efforts. By establishing an agreed measure at the start, not only have you aligned expectations, but you have also enabled objective assessment throughout the project.

MYTH

'It will be obvious that the project has been successful.'

Note that measurement doesn't stop when the project finishes. As we saw in Step 3, quite the reverse is true: managing the ongoing measurement systems is vital to sustaining the change in the long term.

DESTINATION   How will you know Destination is working?

Your team will work on what they think are the priorities, based on their own beliefs and experiences and what they think you and the company expect from them. By having a clearly articulated goal adding value to the customer, and with a well-defined measure and timescale, you will see results quickly as all their efforts will be in the same direction.

Team members will discuss and justify ideas and actions in terms of the goal and the associated measures. Listen to what people are discussing. Does it directly relate to the goal? Are they focused on what the customer needs? Are they assessing ideas against the measure and timescale? When the destination is clear, the answer will be a resounding yes!

It can be dangerous to assume that everyone knows what the goal is. Test it out by asking your team members individually what they think it is. Do they all share the same perspective? And remember, the definition of your final destination is likely to change over time as you progress and learn more. Don't be afraid to revisit it with your team and check with your customers to ensure that your view of the destination continues to meet their needs.

Why Engagement matters

'Coming together is the beginning. Keeping together is progress.
Working together is success.'
Henry Ford

The purpose of engagement is to enable the active involvement of all the people who can help your change be successful.

To engage effectively, you will first identify who needs to be engaged, for what purpose and when, and then ensure a continual flow of communication between all parties. Engagement doesn't commence at the point of implementation; it begins right at the start, with the definition of a shared destination. By continually engaging, you will maintain the focus on a common goal, while adapting your approach to meet the customers' needs.

MYTH

'For a project to be successful, you just need to do a good job on the technical stuff.'

REALITY

People conduct the work; customers receive your product; managers determine priorities and set strategies. In fact, nothing happens without people. The fate of your project will be greatly influenced by others: they have the power to help it to be a great success, or add it to the gigantic mound of project failures.

An engaged team is much more than the sum of its parts, as this Indian parable illustrates.

The story of the elephant and the blind men

Six blind men were asked to describe an elephant by feeling its body.

He who feels a leg says the elephant is like a pillar.

He who feels the tail says the elephant is like a rope.

He who feels the trunk says the elephant is like a tree branch.

He who feels the ear says the elephant is like a hand fan.

He who feels the belly says the elephant is like a wall.

He who feels the tusk says the elephant is like a solid pipe.

A sighted (wise) man explains to them, 'You are all right. The reason each one of you is describing it differently is because you all touched a different part of the elephant. So, actually the elephant has all of the features you mentioned.'

At the start of your project, you will undoubtedly have some understanding of the current situation, but do you fully understand it from the perspective of your customers and suppliers? Or how about the perspective of all the people involved in the process? Just as each of the blind men had their own understanding of the elephant, your suppliers, customers and process operators will all have different insights on what is happening currently and what issues exist. Without combining all of these perspectives, you may create a solution which addresses only part of the problem, or sometimes the wrong problem entirely. Together you can achieve far more than you could individually.

Sam's team found this when they walked through the current process during the Kick-off & Analyse meeting…

Effective engagement requires a clearly defined destination.

DESTINATION   Imagine if I asked you to come on a trip with me, but I didn't tell you where we were going or why we should make the journey. You probably wouldn't be rushing to pack your bags!

Similarly, engagement is much more effective when there is a defined destination and the reason for the change is clear. Don't assume people know the destination; allow time for discussion. Unless people buy in to the need for change, they will never fully engage.

Engagement will smooth the path of your project at every stage:

Align	Analyse & Design	Implement	Run & Learn
Customer and stakeholder input will inform the project selection process and definition of the goal. Their early input will kick start commitment to achieving the goal.	An engaged team will work together effectively to understand the problem and define and implement solutions that really do work.	Engagement can make the difference between launching the change to a hostile, challenging reception or to an informed, supportive environment, where people understand what is happening and why, and feel fully involved.	Stakeholders can be helpful in both anticipating and overcoming obstacles, while also watching out for any surprise changes in the wider environment. Engaging people in the review and learning process will ensure you can replicate success elsewhere.

Establishing productive ways of working and bringing people together for regular working sessions throughout a project will enable everyone to stay aligned and on track.

> *'Boundaries should be meeting places, not dividing lines.'*
> Unknown

We are often reminded that the strength of a chain is determined by the weakest link. Equally in teams, our strength is largely determined by how well we connect and align in service of achieving the overall goal. By strengthening these junctions through positive engagement, we can ensure our teams become exponentially more powerful. In short, engagement is the fast-track to project success.

Engagement is a huge subject which is the sole topic of many books. We are sharing the vital three concepts you can implement quickly which will make a difference to the effectiveness of your engagement.

These three concepts are:

1.   **Seek to understand**

2.   **Power of the positive**

3.   **Make it real**

Let's review these individually.

Seek to understand

'If you make listening and observation your occupation,
you will gain much more than you can by talk.'
Robert Baden-Powell

The purpose of seeking to understand is to make sure that you have taken all perspectives into account so that you can define and deliver the best solutions. To understand, the one essential skill is the ability to listen. This will enhance your progress at every step.

Align	Analyse & Design	Implement	Run & Learn
Listen to your customers to understand what is currently happening and what they really need.	Listen to your team to understand the issues and opportunities.	Listen to those who will be implementing the changes to understand the critical success factors.	Listen to those who are implementing the changes to understand how things are actually working in practice.

When you have a problem, it can be tempting to dive straight into action to fix it, but the most valuable and informative thing you can do at this stage is to:

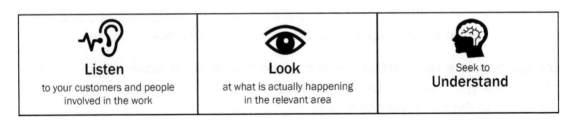

Listen	**Look**	Seek to **Understand**
to your customers and people involved in the work	at what is actually happening in the relevant area	

Use paraphrasing to consolidate and confirm your understanding. This will give you the opportunity to check you have heard correctly and further enhance the dialogue.

📄 **Related tipsheet:** Paraphrasing.

The insights you gather will form the basis for setting a destination and will inform all subsequent decisions on what you choose to do.

'Listening is active. At its most basic level, it's about focus, paying attention.'
Simon Sinek

The listening doesn't stop when you have defined a destination. You and your team need to really pay attention to each other. In this way, you will reveal the subtleties and nuances of what is happening currently. Then, together, you will understand the root causes and piece together solutions that will be truly effective.

EXAMPLE

When Sam's team was working on potential solutions, they discovered that one of these would not be possible in the six-week implementation time. A team member spent time listening to the experts to understand the issue and the alternatives. They then raised the issue with the team, and Sam listened and paraphrased back what she had heard to make sure she had understood the constraint.

'When you talk, you are only repeating what you already know.
But if you listen, you may learn something new.'
Dalai Lama XIV

Once you have carefully designed your proposed solution, it can be tempting to tune out, leave implementation to others and eye up your next exciting project, but this is the make or break point. All your previous work will have been a waste of time if you don't stay completely focused on observing how the changes are being received and what problems people are encountering along the way. There will always be issues, but if you listen carefully to the feedback, you can work with your team and respond accordingly.

EXAMPLE

When Sam's team had implemented the new process, one of the in-process measures highlighted a problem. A team member spent time listening to the people responsible for getting the data the team needed so she could work with them to resolve the issue.

Power of the positive

'If you change the way you look at things, the things you look at change.'
Wayne Dyer

The purpose of the power of the positive is to harness the abundant energy created by positive thinking and channel this to help your project succeed.

What it *isn't*	What it *is*
✗ Assuming a negative comment is a block and the person who is making it is out to cause trouble.	✓ Assuming people have a positive intent in what they are doing or saying, even if they appear to be negative.
✗ Turning a drama into a crisis.	✓ Taking a negative situation and turning it into a positive discussion about how an obstacle can be overcome.

✗ Criticising what people do wrong.	✓ Catching someone doing something right, and recognising it. *'Everyone wants to be appreciated, so if you appreciate someone, don't keep it a secret.'* Mary Kay Ash
✗ Ignoring the negative.	✓ Finding the positive and harnessing that energy to resolve issues.

Would you like every meeting you attend to be more productive, collaborative, friendly and, dare we say it, fun? Well, wish granted! There is actually a remarkably easy way to achieve this.

Start on a positive note. Make sure that the first person to speak talks about positive things in an enthusiastic and inclusive manner. For example, start any meeting with a short summary of all the things that are going well. This doesn't mean glossing over issues, but rather pointing out how problems are being successfully addressed. Encourage laughter and a relaxed atmosphere, and make sure you recognise the contributions of others generously. In particular, highlight successful examples of people working together to solve issues. If you can also throw in some self-deprecating humour, then great.

The unstated message is that this is a team that gets things done; that leaves egos at the door; that has fun while working.

> *'Laughter is the shortest distance between two people.'*
> Victor Borge

The more relaxed people are, the more openly they communicate, and the faster real issues will be raised *and* solved.

EXAMPLE

Sam started the Design meeting by thanking Ash for gathering the data and preparing a Pareto chart of the reasons for non-delivery. She expressed how helpful it was in understanding where the team needed to focus to come up with solutions.

What about when you get into the depths of the discussion and it all gets difficult?

Stop! Do something different/irrelevant/fun...

Often when you get stuck in a discussion, you are literally stuck in a mental rut. By doing something completely different for a short while, you stimulate a different part of the brain, and can then come back to the problem from a different perspective.

Good displacement activities include:

- Change location – try sitting outside for ten minutes
- Go for a 'walk and talk'
- Give the team a fun challenge, eg. identify 100 different uses for a paper clip

You may be feeling sceptical about this, but we urge you to suspend judgement until you have tried it. We have noticed that a displacement intervention is often followed by an intense period of creativity.

Positivity unleashes creativity. In our everyday lives, we spend so much time dealing with issues and problems, so positivity can provide a fantastic shot of energy and momentum. Challenge the team to 'dare to dream' and imagine how things could be better. What would that look like? How would it feel? How would people behave?

EXAMPLE

Sam worked with her team to define the 'ideal' process in the Analyse & Design phase. Up to that point, the team had been busy thinking about the goal purely in terms of reducing the time to resolve customer complaints. Switching to the super-positive mindset of defining the ideal, they realised that actually the ideal for the customer would be to have no cause for complaint in the first place. Subsequently, the team used this insight to provide a more compelling statement of what they were hoping to achieve, which enabled others to better understand and engage.

Defining the ideal can have a wildly liberating effect on a team as they realise that to really satisfy the customer, they need to be working on much more radical improvements. They are inspired to consider game-changing ideas.

REALITY

The trick is to turn things round. If issues arise or people behave in a negative way, turn this round to a positive perspective. When things are going wrong, the 'power of the positive' is perhaps the single most useful concept in your resource bank.

MYTH

'Being positive means ignoring issues.'

Use the power of the positive to avoid and prevent issues. Usually when people seem to be resisting a change, they are actually trying to highlight a significant weakness in your approach. Ignore them at your peril! If you take time to listen, you may see the situation in a whole new light. Ask them to explain their concerns more fully so that you can really understand their cause for concern and explore its potential impact.

Furthermore, they may be willing to help you tackle this weakness in your plans. They may know the key people/technical knowledge/local customs to address the issue and are just waiting for you to ask.

EXAMPLE: SAM USES PARAPHRASING TO RESTATE A CONCERN IN POSITIVE TERMS

'We can't do the postcode checker in six weeks.'	'Thanks for pointing out that the postcode checker will take more than six weeks. It is really important to know that. Is there anything we can do to ensure the postcode is correct within the six weeks we have?'

In fact, employing the power of the positive can help you avoid getting into issues in the first place.

EXAMPLE: PREVENTING ISSUES

In her charity work at an historical house, one colleague enthusiastically thanks children for being gentle with the fragile toys before they have time to do any damage. It is the spirit of catching people doing it right then shining a spotlight on the model behaviour. Or you could try a more direct approach. A sign at a local rugby club reads: 'Don't criticise, volunteer!'

EXERCISE

- If you are already applying this concept in your work, take a few minutes now to reflect on how it is working. Think about any issues that you have encountered. How did you apply the power of the positive and what impact did it have?

- Remember it is a huge boost to team morale to take time to recognise and celebrate the little achievements throughout a project. Have you been celebrating team successes along the way? What difference is this making to the team?

Make it real

'Seeing is believing.'
Unknown

Our level of understanding profoundly changes when we can really see something. The purpose of 'make it real' is to fast-track to this deeper understanding to encourage people to get involved and to make it easy to contribute.

Both of these are descriptions of the same thing – but which would you find more engaging?

By making things real – concrete rather than abstract; tangible rather than invisible; personal rather than detached – you will oil the cogs of engagement and accelerate the progress of your team. Make it visible to encourage people to contribute. You may have the most marvellous ideas, plans or designs, but if they are buried away on a computer, or in the dark recesses of a drawer, it will be hard to get others actively engaged.

You may want to deepen engagement on a particular topic for a number of reasons:

- **To get input.** In the Align phase, Sam put up a wall chart of the draft success report to prompt input and asked people to comment and post sticky notes on it.

- **Increase alignment around a key aspect.** In the Implement phase, Sam created a display of the action plan to help drive alignment on the progress and timelines.

- **Promote awareness.** During Run & Learn, Sam stuck up a large chart of the final output measure to promote awareness of what the team had achieved and to stimulate interest in the approach they'd used.

If you want engagement in something, you need to make it easy for people to see:

- **Prepare for meetings.** Create a large copy of the key documents that you want people to discuss. Then put these up on a wall or on flipcharts and invite everyone to stand up and add their comments, prior to group discussion. This small piece of prework can make a real difference to the quality and quantity of feedback during the meeting.

- **Find good display areas.** To attract attention outside of meetings, it is good to think creatively about where to put your display. Consider some-where slightly unusual, perhaps by the water cooler, or in the restaurant. In this digital age, this can also mean posting something on a website or a shared area online and talking people through it.

EXAMPLE: SARAH'S DASHBOARD

Sarah identified the small team of people who needed to regularly review the dashboard: the owners of the in-process measures; the customer rep; and the IT guy. Then she found an empty wall space near the coffee machine where most of this team tended to congregate at breaks. Sarah got the dashboard assembled on the wall in this area, and then held weekly meetings standing up by the display. It worked well as the team could also grab a coffee and also it sparked quite a bit of interest from other people who just happened to be taking a break around the same time.

Why not try out this approach for yourself?

EXERCISE

To get started, simply identify:

- Something you want to get input on

- What sort of input you are looking for

- Who you want to provide input

- Use this to help identify where your item should be displayed. Finally, define how and when you will gather input and make this clear on the display.

'Writing is easy: all you do is sit staring at a blank sheet of paper
until drops of blood form on your forehead.'
Gene Fowler

Often, we hear people say that having any kind of rough draft is 'so much easier than starting with a blank sheet'. Providing a framework makes it easier for others to contribute. This is your short cut to more productive conversations, meetings and presentations. We have consistently found that providing a framework helps people to focus on sharing their experience and ideas, and avoids confusion about *how* to provide their input. By 'framework', we mean anything tangible which helps people to structure their ideas, information or work.

EXAMPLE FRAMEWORKS
- A template, eg success report, AAR
- A standardised process, eg Success Cycle, standardised timelines
- First draft of a document, eg process diagram, meeting outputs

Frameworks are used constantly throughout the Success Cycle:

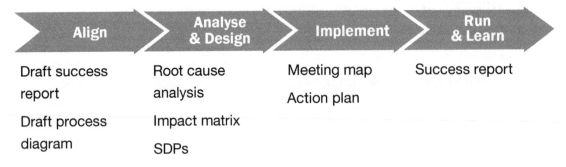

Align	Analyse & Design	Implement	Run & Learn
Draft success report	Root cause analysis	Meeting map	Success report
Draft process diagram	Impact matrix	Action plan	
	SDPs		

Indeed, having a framework helps in multiple ways:

- People can see *what is required*, which also leads to better quality input
- Progress is quicker because people can rapidly work out *how they can contribute*

- Completion is faster because it is easy to *know when to stop*, as you can see when the framework has been filled in

MYTH

'Providing a framework inhibits creativity.'

REALITY

Frameworks *enhance* creative thinking, as people don't waste their time or energy trying to understand what is required. Instead, they can focus all their energies on contributing. You are simply providing the vessel into which they can pour their knowledge and imagination.

There is a further element that will supercharge making it real: make it personal. There are many cultures in which being 'professional' tends to mean being detached or aloof, but the people and interactions that engage and energise us are those where we feel a personal connection.

By seeking to understand others, you can tailor the content of your communications to your audiences' needs and ensure it speaks to their experience. But what about *your* experience? If you reach out from your own personal learnings, this will complete the circuit of connection. Techniques such as storytelling and giving examples from your own experience are useful ways of building involvement.

Another effective way to make it personal is by role modelling the behaviours you are seeking in others.

'Be the change that you want to see.'
Mahatma Gandhi

EXAMPLE: ADOPTING A BEHAVIOUR

If you would like others to use data to make decisions, you might say, 'I have been reflecting on how I can be more effective and realise that sometimes I make important decisions based largely on opinion. Going forward, I want to make sure my choices and decisions are grounded in facts.' Reinforce this whenever the opportunity arises by saying, for example, 'It seems like you think the problem is that we don't have access to the original order details. Can we look at some data to help us better understand?'

 How will you know people are engaged?

We have now explored the three concepts underpinning Engagement – but how will you know that you have been successful in applying them?

You will see:

- People asking lots of questions as they seek to understand, ascertain the impact and evaluate how they can help.

- A free flow of communication which is not bounded by meetings. People will spontaneously discuss the topic and proactively try to move things forward.

- People will feel empowered to take action and be ready to make things happen.

- People will freely articulate how their actions contribute towards the goal.

- Actions are completed on time. People coming to meetings will be prepared and ready to contribute.

- People will happily raise issues, confident in the knowledge that the wider team will support them in finding solutions.

- The wider group of stakeholders will readily share a perspective on the goals and articulate how they will support the project.

Once you see these signs of engagement, you will know you are on the right track. Keep it going and monitor how the engagement is being received.

Now we have explored the principle of Engagement in more depth, let's move on to Iteration.

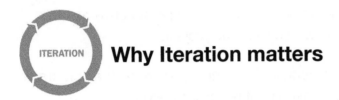

Why Iteration matters

Our final principle is Iteration – rapidly making small incremental changes which will accelerate us towards our destination.

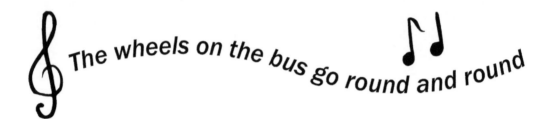

Verna Hill

It's no coincidence that the invention of the wheel is so often cited as a leap forward in human development. Without those speedily revolving wheels, the bus would be stuck, along with the driver and passengers (playing children, chatting mums, knitting grannies…), going nowhere fast. It is the wheels' repeated and rapid iterations that propel them all towards their destination.

The purpose of iteration is to rapidly learn what works in order to accelerate delivery of benefit to the customer. Iteration needs to be rapid. The quicker the cycle of iteration, the sooner you can deliver benefits and learn what works (and what doesn't), and the earlier you can move on with confidence to the next iteration of improvement.

As Sam's team had quickly demonstrated the benefits of improvement in the northern region, they could rapidly move on and gain support for further improvements – both in terms of widening the scope and making new changes.

They delivered benefit to the customer quickly, much earlier than if they had attempted a large change in a single step, and with each iteration the benefit they delivered grew and grew.

EXERCISE

Think about a large project in your business that has long timescales. When will the customer see the benefit of the change? How could you restructure that project to take an iterative approach, where the customer sees at least some of the benefits earlier?

'Great things are done... by a series of small things brought together.'
Vincent Van Gogh

Small iterations deliver big changes. Maybe you are still thinking that small changes don't sound inspiring or even worth bothering with, but incremental change is the best and most reliable way of making a big change. We can see this every day when we look at the natural world – the beautifully elegant and diverse solutions that make up life on our planet are the results of many small changes over time. We can use this approach in our endeavours.

REALITY

One of the 20th century's most iconic achievements – putting a man on the moon – was realised through many rapid iterations. Rockets evolved into satellites, then into multistage craft. Fruit flies were the first space travellers, followed by dogs and monkeys before Yuri Gagarin became the first spaceman. Unmanned missions to the moon paved the way for Neil Armstrong's 'giant leap for mankind' as he stepped onto its surface. Without all the previous iterations, this would have been a mission impossible.

MYTH

'Big changes require big projects and cannot be achieved through rapid iteration.'

Every iteration must focus on the destination. It's important to remember that the wheels on the bus aren't spinning aimlessly; they are driving everyone to their destination. Each improvement iteration meets a short-term goal and each subsequent iteration incrementally drives you towards the long-term destination, the ideal.

The Improvement Journey

Each iteration pushes closer to the overall ideal

Ideal

First project completed

Current Situation

EXAMPLE

In the first iteration of improvement, Sam's team reduced the time to resolve complaints to under 2 days. To build on that initial success, Sarah's team conducted ongoing process reviews, and further iterations moved them closer and closer towards the ideal. They continued to reduce the time taken to resolve complaints and moved towards their long-term ideal destination of no complaints.

Underpinning **Iteration** are three mutually reinforcing concepts:

1. Less is more

2. Learn by doing

3. Use evidence to make decisions

Let's look at each of these in more depth.

Less is more

> *'Perfection is achieved not when there is nothing more to add,*
> *but when there is nothing left to take away.'*
> Antoine de Saint-Exupéry

The purpose of less is more is to create and maintain focus **only** on that which will drive us rapidly towards our destination.

What do we mean by 'less'?

- Fewer resources: *fewer* people, less money and especially time. This last one is known as 'time boxing'.

- Fewer things – the '*vital few*' concepts, solutions or activities.

What it *isn't*	What it *is*
✗ Randomly cutting time or budget	✓ Focusing on the vital few things that will really make a difference

If we look back to the Success Cycle, we can see that as well as applying to the cycle as a whole, this concept is deeply embedded in each individual phase:

Align	Analyse & Design	Implement	Run & Learn
Short-term fixed milestones.

A simple, single goal.

A small team representative of the key process steps. | A small number of time-boxed improvements are selected using just two criteria (impact and time). | Solutions delivered in a fixed time with no extensions – if the plan cannot be achieved, the activities are adjusted rather than the timescale. | A few key measures are monitored to understand the results of the changes. |

'More is not better; more is less; less is more.'
after Mies van der Rohe

It is a common repeating story that we overdo things because we believe that more will be better. At work, how often do we try to address far more issues than we can realistically tackle at one time? When we take on too much, we end up spending a significant amount of time just transitioning from one thing to another as we furiously try to remember exactly what was happening in each situation. This is exhausting and stressful as we constantly feel that we are not really doing a good job of anything.

Constraints make it easier. Focusing on the few things that really matter is the obvious solution, but one that we often struggle to achieve.

The trick is to deliberately constrain the resources available to help us focus. Allocate less time, not more; assign fewer people to the team; allow just one slide for a presentation…

MYTH

'A big problem requires a big budget.'

REALITY

To get that big budget is probably the worst thing that could happen. With a large project, layers of bureaucracy build up to help manage all the different activities so valuable resources get drained away in managing the self-inflicted complexity. This is pure waste masquerading as real work.

It is hard to imagine how a project *can* be successful without embracing the concept of less is more. If we do *more* than the vital few things, we are creating distractions, wasting resources and causing delay, which makes it much harder for the project to succeed.

> *'To achieve great things, two things are needed:*
> *a plan, and not quite enough time.'*
> Leonard Bernstein

Because time is finite, time boxing is an incredibly powerful way of creating a constraint that brings focus and all its attendant advantages. You can apply this trick in all sorts of situations, from meeting agendas to creating project plans.

The traditional way of creating a project plan is to work out the detail of how long each activity will take, put the activities in order and work out the end date. Time boxing requires a different approach: firstly, 'start at the end' and identify the improvement target and delivery date; then, define the high-level plan and milestones to meet these targets. The delivery itself will be easier and quicker.

Remember, you are not simply demanding a shorter timeline; you are also asking the team to reduce the number of things they do by focusing effort on the few important things. Through constraining time in this way, you enable the team to make the hard decisions about what they should, and should not, do.

EXAMPLE

Sam's team had done their root cause analysis and brainstormed different solutions that would help reduce the time taken to resolve complaints. One solution, the postcode checker, seemed to be a great idea – the team thought that it would eliminate a lot of the complaints at source. The only snag was that it couldn't be done within the agreed timescale for the project.

By developing an alternative solution which could be implemented within the timescale, Sam and her team delivered a significant improvement that reduced the number of complaints due to incorrect addresses. They also learnt a lot about what types of address errors customers actually made, which helped them to decide what types of additional checks were needed to gain further improvement.

Putting this into practice isn't always easy and requires a lot of discipline. What if Al and Jo (Sam's sponsor and manager) had thought that delaying the project to implement the postcode checker was a good idea? Or worse, what if they'd wanted to implement all the improvement ideas and not just focus on the vital few? This can happen if a manager or sponsor isn't familiar with the concept of 'less is more'.

In this case, Sam's best plan would have been to show them the evidence that the team had gathered, explain the root causes and demonstrate that this approach would enable the team to make rapid progress towards their goal. Sam had one big advantage: she *could* swiftly demonstrate that this approach works. Al and Jo would be quick to get on board when they saw hard data and improved customer satisfaction.

Another way of focusing on the vital few things is to make this a virtuous habit. In response to any question on priorities, a colleague of ours always states that:

'The three most important things are...'

We used to joke that it was *always* three things, no matter what the context, but in fact what he was doing was maintaining focus.

What are the three most important things for you at the moment? Working out what they are and doing only these things will help you to be successful.

EXERCISE

Think about your objectives. Do you have more than three? If so, which are the vital three that will really make a difference to your business? Agree with your boss which ones are going to be your focus. Then for each of those, what are the few things you can do today to move them towards their destination?

If you haven't already tried time boxing your meetings, see the Quick-start Guide in Step 1 and apply it to your next meeting. See if it makes a difference to the success of the meeting.

Learn by doing

> *'Tell me and I forget. Teach me and I remember. Involve me and I learn.'*
> Benjamin Franklin

The purpose of 'learn by doing' is to quickly gather the best evidence to understand whether a change is effective and gain momentum for improvement.

Trying things out creates the evidence that enables learning. Think of a child learning to walk and talk. They keep on trying things out, repeatedly refining what they do. By continuously attempting new things, they progress from being unable to even turn over to sitting up, to pulling themselves up, taking a few wobbly steps to running. Each time the child tries something new, they create another piece of evidence about what works and what doesn't. If they lean over too far, they will fall. If they put their arm out, it will balance them. All of these collective pieces of evidence combine to enable them to learn and perfect highly complex processes.

Similarly, by trying out our theories about what might improve our process, we too can generate evidence that will determine if we are correct.

EXAMPLE

Sam's team had a theory that by reducing the errors made on the customer's address, they could reduce the number of complaints. They quickly implemented changes to the postcode field on the order form, and then collected data on the number of complaints due to incorrect addresses. This enabled them to gather the evidence to see if their theory was correct.

Note that the team not only had to do the test, but they also had to observe the results to gather the evidence that they needed to see if it was successful.

'Doing' tests out assumptions and theories. In the laboratory, we can perform scientific experiments where we keep all the variables constant, apart from the ones that we are interested in. We can test out what happens to one thing if we change another and collect evidence to support our theories with precision.

Outside of the laboratory, things are not quite so simple. There are many variables that are beyond our control, and some that we won't even know about. The environment that we are introducing our change to and the assumptions that we have made are complex and multifaceted, so the easiest way to find out what actually works is to try things out for real. We will soon find out if our theory is correct.

'Failure is success, if we learn from it.'
Malcolm S Forbes

Of course, the result of testing something out may be that it doesn't work as we thought it might. 'Failure' is often seen as a negative, but in fact it is just evidence that will enable us to learn how to improve. Thomas Edison said that his one thousand failed attempts to invent the lightbulb were the process steps to his ultimate success.

EXAMPLE

Sam's team tested out their daily order listing process and found that it wasn't working as they'd hoped. They were able to identify and fix the root cause of the problem in the data extraction routine and meet their goals of providing the listing within the agreed timeframes.

Testing out theories is informative, but the further step of reflection turns what you have just observed into learning. In our busy lives, we often skip this step – and the eureka moment comes when we are in the shower or during another enforced pause. By building in conscious reflection times, we can deepen our learning.

Another way that we can strengthen our reflection is by sharing it with others. Listening to the perspective of others, can help put our own experiences into context and guide us to that 'Aha!' when we understand something more profoundly.

This understanding can be on two levels. Firstly, the immediate learning from what worked/didn't work in a particular situation. One example of this would be determining whether making a postcode field mandatory does in fact reduce complaints. The next level is a more abstract conceptualisation of what works/doesn't work across different situations. An example of this would be that removing opportunities to make mistakes early in the process avoids downstream rework. Learning is, of course, iterative; the mental models that we build can, and should, be refined over time as we gain more and more experience.

EXAMPLE

Sam's team paid close attention to the review steps they'd built into the process, such as ongoing review of in-process measures. They also built reflection into their standard ways of working by doing regular AARs in their meetings. Their AAR at the close-out meeting at the end of the project reflected on how they might run similar projects in the future.

This is a great example of more abstract learning.

EXERCISE

As we are now reflecting on the principles that we have applied in this book, this is an ideal time to deepen your own learning and reflect on what you have done. If you have tried out some of the suggestions in the Quick-start section in Step 1, reflect on what you have learnt from this experience. If you have gone further and tried a project like Sam's, what have you learnt? What will you do differently next time?

If you haven't done either of these, find another way to see whether 'learn by doing' truly works. For example, you could now try out the AARs detailed in the tipsheets or something else that appeals to you from the book so far. Try learning through reflection on your experience and see what insights you gain.

Use evidence to make decisions

'In God we trust; all others must bring data.'
W Edwards Deming

The purpose of using evidence to make decisions is to make aligned and effective decisions that are:

- Objective – people are aligned by a shared understanding of the data and a conclusion rapidly emerges. It is no longer a case of everyone peddling their favourite theory.

- Transparent – you don't need to construct justification for the decision; the data does the talking for you.

At every stage of a project, you are faced with making important and often seemingly difficult decisions. By collecting evidence, including data and measures, you will be able to take these decisions rapidly and with great confidence.

Align	Analyse & Design	Implement	Run & Learn
Gather evidence on problem and goal.	Use evidence to analyse the problem/ opportunity. Identify root causes.	Use evidence to resolve issues.	Use data to learn what works.

'Errors using inadequate data are much less than those using no data at all.'
Charles Babbage

Often data is not that readily available for poorly performing, ill-defined ways of working. At this point, many teams give up – they think that because there is little or no data, they can skip this activity. They may think that collecting and analysing data will take a lot of time and slow them down.

It is true that collecting and analysing data takes time; the key is to do *just enough* to have a good objective understanding of the situation and then move on. It is not necessary to have every possible piece of data on everything vaguely related to the problem.

MYTH

'We don't have easy access to data, so we should just carry on without it.'

REALITY

Even without a complaint tracking system, Sam's team could still have followed a sample of complaints through all of the stages. The smaller the sample, the higher the risk that it is unrepresentative, but even a small sample will give much more information than none.

You can gather evidence in many ways. For example, the team might obtain a collective opinion, such as customer feedback, and further enhance this by comparing it to relevant data. If the feedback and data are inconsistent, you have a great opportunity to learn.

Consider questions such as 'Are the measures really reflecting customer needs?'; 'Are we collecting feedback from a representative sample of customers?' The answers will not only give insight into your challenge, but also help you define better ways of collecting evidence.

Data is helpful at every stage, particularly at project closure. Have you ever reached the end of a project where the team thinks it has been successful, but the customers don't? Unfortunately, this is all too common.

This can be avoided by collecting evidence and agreeing measures of success with your customer at the *start* of your project. Then you can be confident that everyone will draw the same conclusions at the end.

EXAMPLE

At the end of Sam's project, the sustained change in the agreed output measure demonstrated the team's overall success. The data clearly showed the reduction in the time taken to resolve complaints from a maximum of 10 days to under the target of 2 days.

The use of measures makes the evaluation of project success quick, straightforward, objective and easy to communicate.

Having well-defined measures also makes it much easier to *be* successful. The investment Sam's team made in collecting and analysing data at the start made it easy for them to make decisions in all stages of the Success Cycle.

It is surprising how often apparent disagreements among team members are actually due to a lack of alignment about the problem. When a group of experts comes together, they often feel that they understand the area better than anyone else and already have ideas about what the solution should be to the problem, as they perceive it. A better approach is to use their expertise to define the problem in a measurable way. This will help identify assumptions and misconceptions and allow the team to become truly aligned.

EXAMPLE

Together, Sam's team examined the cycle time data related to the different steps in complaints handling. When they were considering which solutions to develop, it was clear which would have the most impact on complaint resolution time. For example, they could see that stopping the routine conduct of fraud checks would reduce this by an average of 2.5 days.

As well as facilitating decision making, the time they spent collecting and analysing this data was an investment that paid off later in the project, when the solutions delivered the desired level of improvement. This was largely because of the analysis that went in to defining them.

The use of evidence not only improved the speed and quality of the decisions the team made, but also deepened team engagement. They evaluated every idea in exactly the same objective way, which promoted a collaborative environment where they welcomed any idea, no matter how unusual.

When a team goes through this kind of process together, they emerge united in their support for the proposed solution, because they know the process has been thorough and unbiased. All of Sam's team could clearly explain why reducing fraud checks, creating the order listing and changes to the postcode field were the chosen solutions. This ability to articulate the rationale behind proposals really helped with wider engagement, which became ever more important as the proposals were shared with the larger group of stakeholders.

Once a team has been through one iteration of the Success Cycle, they will have established mechanisms to help with ongoing data gathering. Timely access to relevant data enables the team to be super-efficient in their discussions and decisions, and they can progress quickly, confident in the knowledge that they are working on the right thing.

EXAMPLE

Sarah's process review meetings looked at evidence from in-process measures, output measures and customer feedback to assess the current level of performance in resolving complaints and to decide where to focus their improvement efforts.

Once you have gone through several improvement iterations, you may well find that you are monitoring a large number of measures. Generally speaking, the more evidence you have pointing in a particular direction, the stronger your decisions will be – but there is an important caveat to this: the concept of 'less is more' still applies. Each of these measures will require time, effort and energy to collect, analyse, assess and action. At best, it is a distraction to have a large set of metrics; at worst, it can become so confusing that people miss the signals which really matter. The key is always to collect *just enough* evidence to enable you to have a good objective understanding and make effective decisions.

Identify and collect *only*:

- The key measures that matter to the customer
- The key metrics that reflect how well your way of working is performing

---

EXERCISE

The next time you have a decision to make in a meeting, think if there is any data you can bring that would help with the decision. Put it in graphical form, if possible, and circulate it in advance.

 How will you know that you are successful at rapid iteration?

If you have successfully applied this principle, you'll see:

- Rapid step-wise change in the things that matter to your customers
- Your team will have learnt about the specifics of the things that work and don't work to meet your customers' needs
- Your team will have learnt about how to make changes successfully
- You'll be having easy and open discussions that are based on evidence rather than opinion

In fact, your team will think that small and fast is easy and good. This is counterintuitive to many; we are programmed to think that big is better and fast means poor quality. But your team will have learnt from their repeated experience that rapid iteration is one of the keys to success: doing a few small things quickly, learning from what they have done and being guided by hard evidence, reliably propels them towards their destination. But as always, don't take our word for it; try it for yourself and find out.

The power of combining the principles

Having reflected on all of the principles and concepts and how they can be used in practice, you will have a deeper understanding of the individual components of the Success Equation and its application. But, as we outlined in Step 1, the real value and acceleration of success comes from **combining** the principles and concepts.

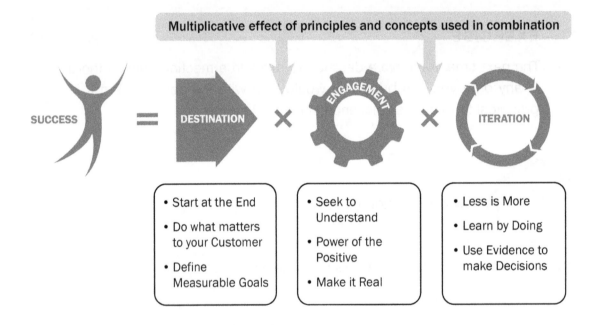

Think back to Sam, right at the start of her project. She had been given a fairly unspecific challenge by her manager, Jo, that complaints were taking too long to resolve. By engaging the key people (the process operators, customers and sponsors) and collecting and using evidence and data, she iteratively built up a clear picture of her destination and was able to describe it as a measurable goal. By applying all of the three principles of the Success Equation together, she set the project up for success.

As the project got underway, Sam had the momentum for action that comes from a team that is already engaged, clarity on the destination and a fixed timeline for delivery of the first iteration of benefit. But what if she'd skimmed over or omitted any one principle? What, for example, if she had done a great job of talking to everyone and getting their views on 'improving complaints', but hadn't defined a measurable goal and agreed it with Al, her sponsor? What would have happened then?

Unfortunately, lack of a clear, agreed goal is a fairly common scenario and leads to some unpalatable risks. You may have personal experience of how hard that type of project can be. Or maybe you have been on a project where the right people were not engaged. Or perhaps you've faced a huge challenge to be delivered over a long timescale.

By disregarding any one of the principles, we introduce a number of serious risks to the project.

Risks due to lack of clear **Destination**:

- Unfocused effort
- Loudest person prevails in getting their way on pet problem and solutions
- Solutions do not benefit the customer

Risks due to ineffectively **Engaging** people:

- Resources are difficult to obtain
- Team members become disaffected
- Operators revert to old methods or solutions

Risks of not completing rapid **Iterations**:

- Benefits take a long time to be delivered, if ever
- It takes a long time to learn anything about which solutions would work
- Spiralling costs and timescales

Maybe you've been on a project where one of these risks became a real issue. Consider how things might have been different with appropriate focus on the relevant principle.

By contrast, if we look back at Sam's project, we can see many examples where the principles worked *in combination* to *accelerate* success. Here are just a few small examples:

- Recapping on the destination and timelines at the beginning of each meeting provided regular reinforcement of how to prioritise activities. Sam focused discussion of issues by asking, 'How will this affect our destination?' and she made rapid iteration possible by repeatedly asking, 'What can we do in the time available?' Remember that when Sam's team found that they were unable to implement the postcode checker within the timeline, they still delivered an impressive benefit to their customers by implementing a smaller change.

- By starting at the end with the draft success report, Sam's team was always clear on what remained undone. They could see that each phase of the Success Cycle was bringing them closer to completion, and this clarity made it easy for them to engage and align on what they still needed to do.

- The SDP owners mocked up the in-process measures during the Analyse & Design phase of the Success Cycle before they were used in the Run & Learn phase to monitor implementation of the changes. Starting at the end made it easy to define the actions needed to collect and report the data. By making these actions real, Sam found it easy to engage the team to iteratively improve the measures. This first iteration provided a great foundation for further improvement as the team 'learnt by doing' to find out what did and didn't work.

It is this **combination** of the three principles that turns them from being individually useful to **exponentially powerful**. Put together, they will propel you to success.

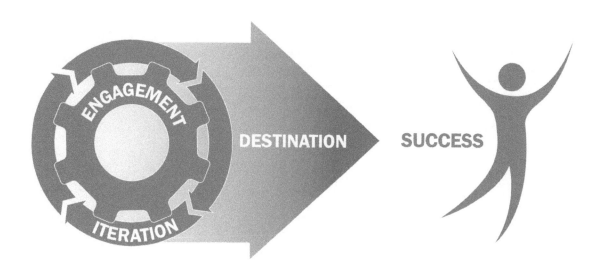

Engagement turns the cycle of **Iteration** that propels you towards your **Destination,** leading to **Success**

STEP 5 – Looking Ahead To The Ultimate Destination

'Success is not final, failure is not fatal: it is the courage to continue that counts.'
Winston Churchill

We have followed Sam all the way from her fledgling steps in collecting some data, drafting a success report and forming a team, to delivering a significant change and establishing long-term processes for ongoing improvement. Sam has certainly been on quite a journey. Hopefully, you have also tried out some of the approaches for yourself and have been reflecting along the way on how using the principles of the Success Equation can help you and your team be successful.

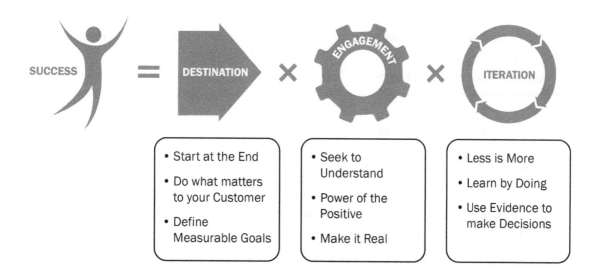

But what if *everyone* in your organisation was using these principles? What if this was the normal way of working? What would that be like?

Let's take a minute and think about how it would be different.

Before	After
'I'm sorry, I can't do anything about your problem till at least next year.'	'We will deliver a significant improvement within six months.'
'I have too many competing issues to deal with yours.'	'We will deliver improvements in the three areas that are most important to our customers this year.'
'I have no idea what the people who provide the service are doing, but I am fed up that nothing seems to be done about my problems.'	'I'm certain that the service team are working on the right things to improve.'
'I can't do anything without a big budget and it will take ages to get approval for the spend.'	'We are confident that we will be able to make a significant change with minimal resources.'
'People who don't know what is happening in my area are making decisions about how best to do my job.'	'There's a great opportunity to improve – let's get started.'

This would lead us to a situation where:

- *More* people develop expertise in applying the Success Cycle, so benefits would be delivered rapidly to *more* customers

- People become more skilful in identifying improvement opportunities, so the amount of benefit they deliver would be larger

- Customers know that their needs are being prioritised

- Managers know that it's not necessary to invest large sums to deliver results, so costs would be low

- Everyone feels valued as their knowledge and experience would be recognised and used, inspiring and motivating them to deliver further success

This is the ultimate destination:

A self-sustaining system that rapidly, reliably and repeatedly delivers lasting business results through a skilled and motivated workforce.

Making this vision a reality doesn't happen overnight; it requires a lot of iterations and focus over a sustained period. To sustain and nurture this process is clearly a major undertaking which is beyond the scope of this book, but like all journeys, it is possible to get started with just a few small steps.

Think back to when you and your team started your journey; when no one had used the Success Equation principles before. There was no common language, no established processes, no experience to fall back on when things went wrong. People didn't know what was expected of them and hesitated to commit support. They might have lacked confidence in the outcome and were questioning if it was worth the effort.

But once people try it for themselves and understand what applying the Success Equation means and the potential benefits, all of these issues melt away. And with each iteration of the improvement cycle, there will be a growing number of people who have personal experience and their own learnings. And if each person passes on something that they have learnt to others, the Success Equation principles will proliferate. The more people who know what using the principles can achieve and how to use them, the easier it will become, and the change will accelerate towards becoming self-sustaining.

You can personally do a few small things to start your organisation on the path towards the ultimate destination:

- **Make it personal.** If you put the principles and supporting concepts into practice at every opportunity, you will visibly demonstrate to others what it takes to be successful. Encourage and support those who want to emulate you.

- **Communicate your success.** Find ways to let people know about the great things that you and your team have achieved. Talk about the benefits you have delivered and describe your experience of what it took to get there. This will be a powerful way of creating 'the pull' for people to want to try out the Success Equation for themselves.

- **Engage senior management.** As you continue to apply the Success Equation and consistently deliver benefit to your customers, be ready to take advantage of questions and interest from senior management. They can really help pave the way towards a self-sustaining system.

As you travel towards the ultimate destination, the Success Equation will continue to inspire and guide you. It doesn't matter if you are just starting to explore the principles or have used them for many years; whether you've completed one iteration or many; whether you've spread the word in one small team or across a multinational company. Wherever you are on your journey, the three principles of **Destination, Engagement and Iteration** will work together to lead you along the path to success.

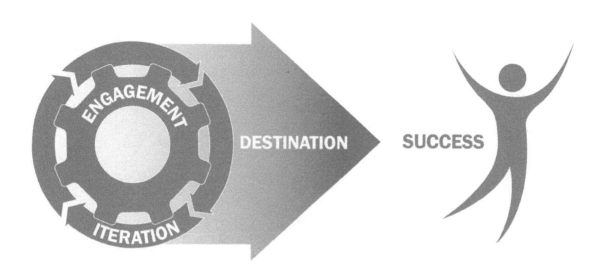

Engagement turns the cycle of **Iteration** that propels you
towards your **Destination,** leading to **Success**

So now you have the equation for success, where are you going to start?

PART 2

Success Equation Resources

Introduction

In Part 1, we explained the Success Equation and explored how to apply the principles to challenges of all shapes and sizes. In particular, we illustrated how to apply the Success Equation to a larger challenge using the Success Cycle methodology as we followed Sam through a complete case study.

The second part of the book contains a wealth of materials to guide and support you in addressing your own challenges, both large and small, using the Success Equation principles. As with most things, there is a wide variety of different tools and techniques you could use, but many of these share a core set of basic approaches. Here you will find simple, quick versions of the vital few things which will enable you to tackle most situations with confidence and get results.

Special Topics. There are a number of key aids to applying the Success Equation. Here we review these in more detail in order to help you understand them at a deeper level and apply them effectively. These are the topics which we most often find ourselves delving into as we coach people through their projects.

Success Cycle User Guide. Here we describe in detail the structured methodology of the Success Cycle. This in-depth guidance will support you in applying the success principles to your business challenge. It includes specific notes on how to run the series of key meetings which underpin the methodology and ultimately enable the team to meet their goals.

Success Report. This is a worked example of the report you will deliver when you apply the success principles to a specific business goal. It shows you the final outcome of Sam's project.

Sustaining Success User Guide. This is in-depth guidance on how to use the Success Equation principles to sustain the initial success you achieve from your first application of the Success Cycle.

Tipsheets. These are short guides on specific tools and techniques that we typically use when applying the Success Equation and Success Cycle.

Help, I'm Stuck. This is a practical guide on what to do if you hit one of the common problem scenarios. We have based this section on the issues we encounter during our coaching.

Reading List. Our favourite books which have inspired and enlightened us along the way.

The Success Cycle. The overview diagram summarising the key aspects of the Success Cycle for ease of reference.

The Success Equation. The overview diagram summarising the key elements of the Success Equation for ease of reference.

Special Topics

Increasing engagement in meetings

Facilitating a meeting to get the best engagement and contribution from all attendees is a skill that takes much practice. Here is a quick summary of the approaches that we have found to work well.

Create a framework beforehand

We provide plenty of examples of frameworks throughout this book. If you need to develop or adapt one, apply one of our favourite concepts: start at the end. Think about what you want by the end of the meeting/presentation/project, or piece of work, and define what attributes the output should have. Then define a framework which will deliver the output you desire.

The fastest way to ensure a framework is fit for purpose is to test it out, ie learn by doing.

EXAMPLE

One of the tools Sam used in the Analyse & Design stage was fishbone analysis (see the special topic: 'Analysing root causes'). She set this up using standard headings she had found on the internet: Methods, Machines, Manpower, Materials, Measurement. This was a good starting point as it enabled the team to quickly grasp the purpose and process for using this type of analysis. Once the team got going, they applied more specific headings for their particular problem.

If you want people to contribute ideas, don't make the display look polished. Highly professional presentations are for things you have finished when you simply want to inform people what you and your team have done. If you want people to engage, deliberately make it look like a work in progress – something people can contribute to and help develop. For example, you might create your process diagram on a flipchart using sticky notes so the team can move them around as they work on it.

Creating a framework can take time. For example, doing the prework to carefully design a meeting agenda and associated template for the participants to complete during the meeting will be a significant time investment. Think of developing a framework as a mark of respect to the people you want to engage. You want to ensure that every minute of the time they spend on your project is focused and productive.

 Related tipsheet: Meeting maps.

Start strong

It is widely known that in personal interactions, first impressions count. We believe the same is true for meetings – you have just a couple of minutes to establish that your meeting will be interesting and worthwhile. After that, it will be an uphill struggle to get everyone to fully engage.

The start of the meeting needs to quickly establish answers to the following questions for all of the meeting attendees:

Questions	How to answer
What is the purpose of the meeting?	Apply the concept 'start at the end'. A quick review of the planned outputs for the meeting will establish what it aims to achieve. Make sure you explicitly check that people agree with these outputs. You need to address any misunderstanding or confusion *before* starting the discussion.
Why am I here?	Is it obvious why each individual is in the room? You may need to state this explicitly, for example '…and the reason we have Linda here today is because she is an expert on the IT system we are using and will be able to give some initial feedback on the practicality of our proposals.'
Do I want to be here?	Too many meetings are long, boring and impersonal. Make yours different: • Greet everyone personally as they arrive. • Encourage laughter and an informal atmosphere. It is always great if you can start a meeting with some humour. • Set timings on the agenda and stick to them.

Generate some energy

When you put something up on a wall, generally people are standing up when they review it. This immediately helps with engagement. Standing up stimulates the mind into thinking it needs to do something, and you can direct that energy towards engagement in your project. You can also change the relative positions of people in the room more easily when they're standing up.

Note how in a formal presentation, the speaker stands and faces a seated audience; when everyone stands up, they become one group working side-by-side. This small change can completely change the tone of discussion from adversarial to collaborative.

EXAMPLE

When you are updating your sponsor, a great technique to increase their engagement is to put the key workings of the team up on a wall and 'walk the walls' with the sponsor. Invite them to contribute their understanding and perspective by giving them a sticky notepad and a pen, or you could write down their observations for them and post them up as you go to illustrate that they are actively helping develop the work of the team.

Keep people aligned

You may have to intervene in the conversation to keep people aligned and on topic. For instance, if people raise an issue:

- Paraphrase (see tipsheet: 'Paraphrasing') to make sure you have correctly understood the problem being raised
- Reconfirm the goal (of the meeting or project)
- Ask, 'How does this issue affect our destination?'
- If it has a significant impact, align the team on resolving it by asking, 'How can we resolve this and make sure we meet our goal?'

Make decisions quickly

In meetings, especially those with a large number of participants, inviting comments from everyone can lead to a lot of old arguments being rehashed with nothing new being said. Red, amber, green (RAG) is a quick way to move discussions on, while ensuring that everyone can participate and serious concerns are heard.

EXAMPLE

Ask all participants to give a status of red, amber or green, where:

- Green = go. I fully support the proposal; we should proceed.

- Amber = concerns. I have some minor concerns, but am OK to proceed without further discussion.

- Red = stop. I can't support the proposal as it stands; I have issues that will need to be addressed before it can go ahead.

You can do this by simply asking, or use flash cards or meeting status indicators in video meetings to aid you. Based on the temperature check, proceed accordingly. If you get all green and/or amber responses, you can proceed without further discussion. Any red responses need to be addressed. Ask individuals to summarise their concerns; consider if it is possible to quickly refine the proposal so that it is acceptable. Alternatively, ask for the person with concerns to collaborate with the proposer to further develop the proposal and resubmit at another meeting.

Sometimes it can be helpful to use the approach of a **working decision**. There can be many reasons why a team is struggling to make a decision. For example, they may not really like any of the options or may not be in agreement over which is the best.

Adopt one of the options as a working decision and commit to review this when more information is available or someone has a better idea. This 'unsticks' the team and allows them to move forward.

It is surprising how successful this approach is. New and better options often simply emerge later and the team can then adopt these quickly and easily, because they gave themselves the *flexibility* of making a working decision. The key to success here is to keep everything transparent. Record the outcome as a working decision and commit to review it later.

For example, when we were writing this book, we went with a working title until a better one spontaneously emerged in a later discussion.

Get the team to reflect on their learning

Always carry out a quick AAR at the end of a meeting. Getting feedback on what worked and what you need to improve as soon as you have completed the main agenda is the quickest way for the team to learn how they can develop their ways of working. Encourage a sense of shared learning and development so that everyone has a feeling of *personal* responsibility for helping meetings to be as effective as possible.

> 📄 **Related tipsheet:** AAR.

Using cycle time as a measure

Our approach to ensuring success is informed by data. Our concepts 'define measurable goals' and 'use evidence to make decisions' depend on the collection and analysis of relevant data, but it can be difficult to know where to start. The purpose of this special topic is to illustrate how and why you can often use cycle time as a simple and effective focus for improvement – not only in time, but cost and quality too.

Cycle time is the total elapsed time for something to be completed/delivered. The first step in using cycle time is to define the start and end points. These are often linked to key customer milestones, for example start point: customer places order; end point: customer receives product.

When you improve cycle time, it means that you deliver the product or service to the customer more quickly. This is a great starting point for improvement.

Studying cycle time reveals issues

The next step is to collect data to find out what the total cycle time is and what is causing it to be so long. We invariably find the same picture:

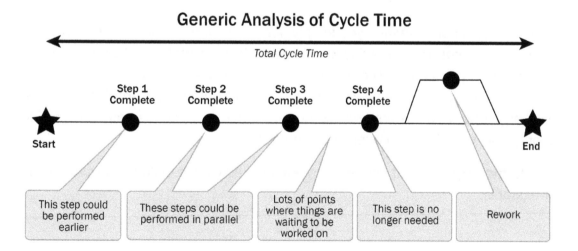

In fact, we can simplify this analysis right down to:

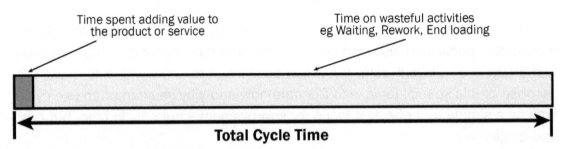

'Adding value' includes just one thing: the time spent adding value to the inputs/ raw materials to create the final output. Wasteful activities include many things and usually account for the vast majority of the total cycle time. This is exciting! It means that there is a massive opportunity for improvement. And we see the same sort of picture over and over again; this is normal.

It may seem surprising that cycle times are so inflated. This is because few processes are consciously designed with the goal of minimising cycle time. A key concept here is the critical path: this is the sequence of activities which take place between the defined start and end points. Most processes have simply evolved over many years to include all sorts of miscellaneous steps on the critical path, causing prolonged cycle times.

To make huge improvements, you simply need to be smarter in how you organise the work. It is *not* about making people work harder; that is not an effective or sustainable approach to improvement. To make show-stopping improvements, all you need to do is tap into the limitless resource of human intellect. By creating a team of people who understand the current process, it will be easy for them to identify how to make the *process* work harder.

Let's further explore what we mean by wasteful activity. It includes several things, for example:

Wasteful activity	Definition	Examples
Waiting time	A work item is waiting to be processed.	Time spent waiting for a part to be supplied.
Rework	Mistakes made earlier in the process take time to be put right.	Product fails an inspection. Report rejected by reviewer.
End loading	Time spent doing things which could have been completed off the critical path.	Designing an analysis *after* the final piece of data has been received.

Top tips:

- We have found that long cycle times tend to have these three generic root causes: waiting, rework, end loading. Using these three categories to prompt your root cause analysis can provide a reliable short cut to identifying the key issues.

- Collect more data to investigate how the total cycle time is subdivided among contributing activities. This analysis quickly identifies the most time-consuming activities and highlights where to focus improvement to achieve the goal.

- Use our generic categories to generate improvement ideas. Simply brainstorm ideas under the following headings:
  - » Reduce or eliminate waiting time
  - » Reduce or eliminate errors that cause rework
  - » Move steps off the critical path or do them in parallel

Typically, an improved process has the following features:

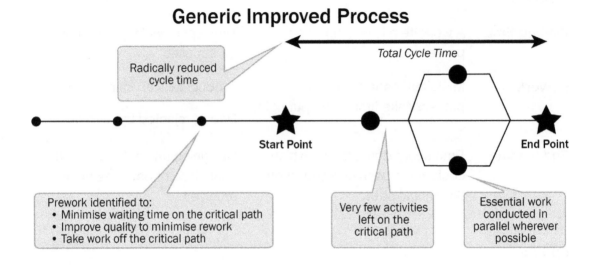

Generic Improved Process

Radically reduced cycle time

Total Cycle Time

Start Point

End Point

Prework identified to:
• Minimise waiting time on the critical path
• Improve quality to minimise rework
• Take work off the critical path

Very few activities left on the critical path

Essential work conducted in parallel wherever possible

EXERCISE

Reflect on how these approaches have been applied to Sam's project. If you look carefully at the new process, you will find the team has taken activities off the critical path, improved quality to reduce rework and reduced waiting time.

Note: it is important not to sub-optimise, ie reduce the cycle time for one process at the expense of another. This is yet another reason for working closely with your customer to ensure that what you're delivering from the new process continues to meet *all* of their requirements.

Cycle time is a great starting point

There are many measures you could use, for example, a measure of quality, such as number of defects or some aspect of cost, which may seem more appropriate, but we recommend using cycle time to define your measurable goal, at least for the first iteration of improvement, because:

- It is easy to measure – just record the total time between the start and end points of your process.

- It is easy to understand and communicate to others.

- Improving cycle time will lead to improvements in other aspects. This is because the causes of long cycle times are also the causes of poor quality and high cost, for example poor communication and lack of preparation.

Remember that Sam used the cycle time to resolve customer complaints as the measure for the first iteration of improvement. Note how this led to a reduction in not only cycle time, but also the number of complaints. Once you have completed your first cycle of improvement, you will have a much deeper understanding of both the process and your customers' needs. Then you will be in a better position to develop and redefine your measures, based on actual experience.

You may have noticed that Sam used *maximum* cycle time to define her target but also used *average* cycle time to analyse what was going on in the process. By using maximum for the target, she engaged people in understanding just how bad the process can get for the customer. When analysing the process, though, you will find it easier to work with averages to identify the most time-consuming sub-processes. In essence, your aim is to reduce both, bringing down the average cycle time and the range of cycle times experienced by the customer.

Collecting and reporting data

The use of data underpins many principles, concepts and activities in this book, particularly 'define measurable goals' and 'use evidence to made decisions'. This special topic will help you to define what data to collect and understand how to collect and display it effectively so that it answers your questions.

What data do you need?

When you're deciding what data to collect, the place to start is, of course, at the end – what do you want to find out? The question that you are trying to answer will depend on where you are in the process improvement cycle – for example:

At the beginning of the Align phase:	'Just how big is this problem – what is the current performance of the process?'
During the Analyse & Design phase:	'What are the root causes that are leading to poor performance?'
During the Run & Learn phase:	'Are the changes working as intended?'
After your first cycle of improvement:	'Is my process performance meeting my customer's needs consistently over time?'

Once you have defined the question, you will be able to define what data to collect to help to answer it.

Collecting data

In the early stages of a new project, data may not be readily available. The process that you are analysing may not have been studied before. If you have an IT system for the process, it may not collect or report the information that you want.

Don't despair – remember that decisions you make using imperfect data are much better than those you make using no data at all, so make full use of the data that *is* available. If you don't have data on the whole end-to-end process, take a sample of pieces of work (complaints, products, reports etc), track them through the process and record the data that you need. For example, one of us once spent several hours working through old emails to track a process at the beginning of a project.

Reporting data

When you're reporting data, there are two basic rules:

Rule #1: Report *all* of the data	Rule #2: PLOT the data
All data is valuable; if you throw data away, you are throwing away information. Sometimes, people will say things like, 'Well, we can exclude Tuesday's data because that day wasn't really typical…' The more useful approach here is to keep the data and annotate the chart with a comment about what happened that was unusual.	It is absolutely amazing how much more revealing a chart can be than a list or a table. A chart showing data over time will quickly reveal patterns and trends, and the scale and duration of changes. It is good to annotate the chart to highlight what it is telling you. Charts need to be living documents, posted somewhere that everyone can easily access. This is not something to be filed in a drawer and brought out once a quarter to show to management.

Plotting the data – the three most useful types of chart:

Question	Chart	When used	More information
What is the performance of my process and how does it/will it change with time?	Performance chart (also known as a run chart)	Throughout the Improvement cycle	See tipsheet 'Performance chart'
Which categories are the biggest cause of my problem?	Pareto chart	Analyse & Design phase	See tipsheet 'Pareto charts'
Are the changes we have implemented working as desired?	In-process measure chart	Run & Learn Phase	See tipsheet 'In-process measures'

Indeed, it is hard to overstate the importance of the performance chart. This is fundamental to the success report so must be updated regularly throughout the project. It is also used after the project has been completed to manage the process over the longer term.

Going forward

As you progress through the project and into managing your process in the longer term, you will learn more about what information is valuable to you. Once you have learnt from real experience what is useful, make the processes of data collection and reporting as automated as possible. Remember that data needs to be collected in *real time* so that you can use it to take proactive action. The more that you can automate, the more you can focus your valuable time on reviewing reports, not creating them.

Beware! It can be easy to get carried away by data. Sometimes people think they need to capture data on every possible aspect of the process, but this comes at a cost: it takes time to review and manage data. Apply the concept of 'less is more'; start with a few measures, see how they work, then modify them as you learn more about the process and your customers.

Analysing root causes

Root cause analysis is a structured method for understanding and verifying the underlying causes of a problem or undesirable outcome. This approach is an important part of 'use evidence to make decisions'. We use this type of analysis within the Success Cycle because it enables teams to design robust solutions, confident in the knowledge that they are addressing the real problem and not just the symptoms. The purpose of this special topic is to help you to apply this technique to your problem.

Root cause analysis can be used for any problem that has been clearly defined. Within the Success Cycle, we use it in the Analyse & Design phase.

There are three key steps to analysing root cause:

1. Determine potential root causes

2. Form theories about the potential root causes

3. Use data to pinpoint and verify potential root causes

Determine potential root causes

This step helps you gain alignment through visually representing and consolidating the issues causing the problem, and then using logical deduction to further explain why they happen.

Fishbone analysis:

- As a team, start with the problem statement and put this on the right-hand side of a large piece of paper or flipchart.

- Identify some broad categories that may be causing the problem (eg Materials, Methods, Machinery, Measurement, People, Environment) and draw a 'bone' (line) for each of these.

- Systematically go through each category to think about what could be causing the problem. This is done by repeatedly asking, 'How does (this category) contribute to this (problem statement)?' Capture each idea on a sticky note and then add it to the 'bone' for that category. You may add smaller bones to capture the next layer of detail.

- When you've captured all ideas, you will have documented many *possible* causes of the problem. To proceed, work out which are the *vital few* causes generating *most* of the problems. For example, the team members could each vote independently on what they think are the top three things causing the problem, based on their experience and observations of working closely in this area.

EXAMPLE: A SECTION OF SAM'S FISHBONE ANALYSIS

Not enough staff

Warehouse operators in a hurry

Ordered wrong book

Not expecting parcel

Customer inputs wrong address

Customer hasn't seen the parcel

Customer not in

Everyone does the process differently

Customer mistakes

PEOPLE

Problem statement: UK book complaints take average 5 days, max 10 days to resolve

Call handlers not clear on what to do

METHODS

Customer info is wrong

Too many complaints to handle

Checking for previous claims

Address errors

Poor training

Similar name at same address eg flats

Incorrect address

Fraud checks take ages

Lots of different complaint types

Their top three possible causes were:

1. The delivery address is often incorrect

2. Customers often input the wrong address on the internet order form

3. The fraud checks take a long time

Don't assume that the causes you and your team brainstorm from the fishbone analysis are the root causes. Always make sure you use the 5 Whys to drill down deeper.

Form theories about the potential root causes

Use the 5 Whys to drill further down into the top issues you've identified to get to the underlying cause of the problem. For each of the most likely causes, ask, 'Why does this cause <problem statement>?' Then ask the same question of the response. Do this up to five times until you have an actionable cause.

EXAMPLE: SAM'S TEAM'S 5 WHYS (EXTRACT)

Why do UK book complaints take an average of 5 days and a maximum of 10 days to resolve?

1. Because the delivery address is often incorrect.

   Why does the incorrect delivery address cause book complaints to take a long time to resolve?

   Because the complaints handler has to check the address on the order.

   Why does checking the address on the order cause book complaints to take a long time to resolve?

   Because the complaints handler has to ask the sales team for the original address information.

   Why does having to ask the sales team for the original address cause book complaints to take a long time to resolve?

   Because the complaints handler does not have direct access to the order system and has to wait for the sales team to provide this information.

   This is an actionable cause.

2. ....

Sam's team carried on with this approach, analysing the root of each of the three causes they had selected from their fishbone diagram. Based on this, the **team's potential root causes** for why UK book complaints take an average of 5 days and a maximum of 10 were:

- The complaints handler does not have direct access to the order system
- The address entered by the customer is not validated at the time of entry
- The fraud checks are done for all customers and take a long time to do

Use data to pinpoint and verify potential root causes

Once you have identified your potential root causes, they become your theories of what is causing the problem you're investigating, but it can be a mistake to assume that the causes you first think of are correct. It is always best to collect some evidence to verify or disprove your theories so you don't waste time designing solutions that won't solve the problem. Define the data you need to do this and assign actions among your team.

Once you have the data, organise and present it in a way that confirms or disproves your root causes. Pareto charts and cycle time analysis are often useful here. For more information, see the tipsheet: 'Pareto chart' and the special topic: 'Using cycle time as a measure'.

Example: Sam's team collected the following data:

Data collected	Summary of the data
Cycle times for getting the order information.	Getting order information takes on average 1.5 days.
Cycle time for fraud checks.	Fraud checks take on average 2.5 days.
Reasons for non-deliveries.	70% of non-deliveries are caused by incorrect address. Fraud checks account for only 1% of non-deliveries.

Sam's team used the data to verify that their theories of the root causes were highly probable, and if they could address these issues, they could be confident the process would be greatly improved.

Note: it may be possible to collect data in advance to enable all three steps to be completed during the Kick-off & Analyse meeting. For example, you may already have a breakdown of the sub-steps of a cycle time measure.

To summarise, root cause analysis is a rigorous analytical approach to understanding the problem you are investigating. It provides a solid foundation for developing improvement ideas, and a fast and efficient technique to guide your subsequent choices and actions. Furthermore, collaboration on this analysis is a powerful way to align and motivate the team, who can then clearly communicate the rationale behind their proposals.

Success Cycle User Guide

Introduction

In Step 2 we went through Sam's case study, which illustrated, at a high level, how to apply the Success Cycle to rapidly deliver beneficial change. This User Guide is a more practical guide on how to apply the Success Cycle to your situation.

You may remember the overview diagram for the whole cycle:

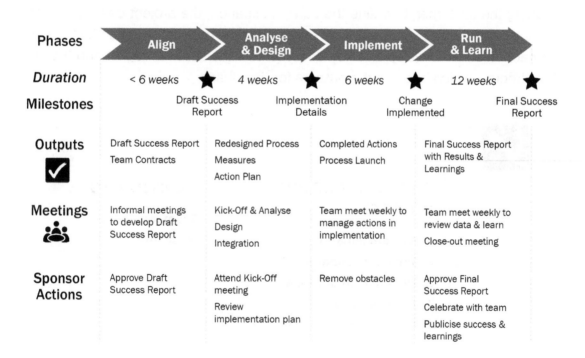

We are now going to explain the Success Cycle in detail and go through exactly how to develop the outputs needed from each phase. We will also go through how to run each of the specific meetings, so that they deliver the outputs you require and engage the team while rapidly moving forward towards your **Destination**.

Phase 1: Align

Phases	Align	Analyse & Design	Implement	Run & Learn
Duration	< 6 weeks ★	4 weeks ☆	6 weeks ☆	12 weeks ☆
Milestones	Draft Success Report	Implementation Details	Change Implemented	Final Success Report

The Align phase is the start of your improvement journey towards customer satis-faction and long-term prosperity. At this initial stage, it is vital you collaborate effectively to ensure all your key stakeholders are fully on board. Specifically, this means that you need to reach agreement with the sponsors and key stakeholders, including the customer, to define the current situation, the project destination, an outline plan and how everyone will be engaged in the project. The practical way to approach this is to develop two key documents – the success report and the set of contracts – which become the outputs for this phase:

SUCCESS REPORT (DRAFT)

1. **Current situation** ✔
2. **Project destination** ✔
3. **Project plan outline** ✔
4. Implementation details
5. Sustaining the change

CONTRACTS

Team members
Sponsors

These documents have been carefully designed to promote focused discussion on the key topics which need to be agreed at this early stage. Completing the documents will be the logical outcome of full **Engagement** with the relevant parties.

How to draft the success report

Drafting the success report at this early stage is a great example of using 'start at the end', one of our key concepts within the principle of Destination. Even at this stage, we can create the first three sections of the success report: current situation, project destination and project plan outline. Initially, this may seem challenging, but we would like you to see for yourself how this is both possible and extremely helpful. As you engage your team and other stakeholders in crafting the report, you will find that you rapidly gain alignment and momentum.

Let's go through each of these three sections, using Sam's project to illustrate what each might look like.

Success report Section 1: Current situation

The first section outlines the problem from the customer's perspective and describes how things are currently operating. Here is an example from Sam's project:

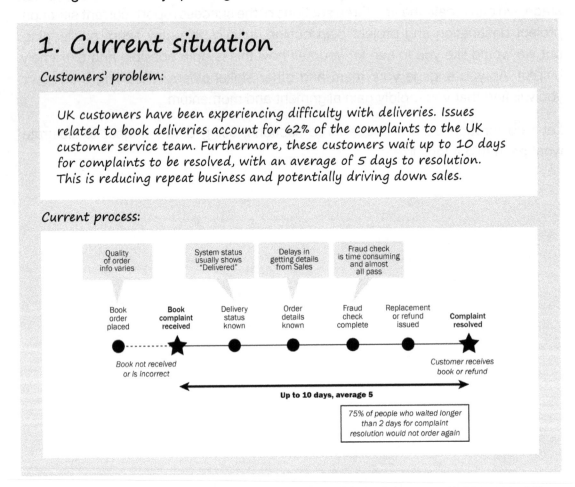

1. Current situation

Customers' problem:

UK customers have been experiencing difficulty with deliveries. Issues related to book deliveries account for 62% of the complaints to the UK customer service team. Furthermore, these customers wait up to 10 days for complaints to be resolved, with an average of 5 days to resolution. This is reducing repeat business and potentially driving down sales.

Current process:

Customers' problem. Before you try to fix a problem, it is essential to spend time clarifying exactly what that problem is, particularly with reference to your primary customers. This is an example of the Destination concept: 'do what matters to your customer'. Your customers are those who directly receive your product or service.

How do you find out what matters to your customers?

- **Ask them,** 'If you could change just one thing about what we deliver, what would you choose?'

- **Observe** how they use what you provide – people get used to the work-arounds that they use and may not even realise that they are doing them.

- **Look at data.** A good starting point is to collate data to determine the current level of performance and assess that in relation to customer requirements. You may have additional data, perhaps on the types and frequency of customer complaints. Sometimes it isn't so obvious – maybe the number of iterations of a draft, or the number of complaints that never get answered.

This is a great time to apply the Engagement concept: 'seek to understand'. It requires honest discussion, particularly with your customers, to get insight and alignment on what is really happening. To practise and improve your listening skills, try paraphrasing what you have heard. This discussion is an iterative process – summarise what you have learnt and take it back to your customers until you have it right.

Together, prioritise which of their needs you are going to focus on first and consolidate this into a simple statement of the problem and the impact it has. The statement must include data on how big the problem is. Without data, you won't be able to objectively evaluate the level of success.

> 📄 **Related tipsheets:** Defining your customer; Paraphrasing.

Current process. By process, we mean a series of actions or steps taken in order to achieve a particular end. A process will have a defined output, a number of steps that will achieve that output, and some inputs that are transformed into the output. The current process diagram in the success report is a simple illustration of the process that you are aiming to change and what you think is wrong with it. The goal of creating this diagram is to establish a common understanding of the problem and the issues that cause it.

Creating this diagram needs to involve customers and the people doing the work so that it truly represents the current process, not some idealised version as understood by management. Creating the process diagram will also help you to gather the information that you need to scope your change and build your team. Gathering the details of what is currently happening to inform how the project is defined is a good example of the Iteration concept: 'use evidence to make decisions'.

> 📄 **Related tipsheet:** Process diagram.

Success report Section 2: Project destination

The second section outlines what the project aims to achieve, describing the goal both in words and graphically. Here is an example from Sam's project:

2. Project destination

Goal statement:

> Reduce complaint resolution time for the northern region from a maximum of 10 days to a maximum of 2 days by 4 July.

Performance chart:

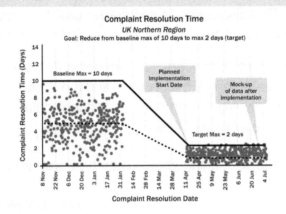

Note: this chart gets updated with actual data during Run & Learn.

Remember that 'define measurable goals' is a key concept within Destination. Having a well-defined Destination will be a constant source of inspiration throughout the project and will act like a guiding light when the going gets tough.

Goal statement. This is a simple statement quantifying the aim of the improvement. In fact, it is a summary of the key elements of the performance chart and can't be finalised independently. The statement needs to:

- **Be specific and measurable:** make your target ambitious and in line with what your customer needs, rather than what you think might be achievable.

- **Define scope:** This identifies the subset of work where you will focus to get the most impact and learning on this first iteration. Remember less is more. Making the scope explicit early on helps you to work out who you need to involve in the change.

- **Set the date:** Specify the planned date that you expect to demonstrate real improvement. We will talk more about timescales later under 'Project plan outline', but for now, think about keeping them relatively short and visible on the horizon.

Top tip: consider using cycle time as the primary measure.

Note the goal should not contain how it will be achieved; you're looking for the strategy at this stage, not the tactics.

 Engagement is key in the development of the goal. This requires extensive liaison with your sponsor and key stakeholders, including the people who work in the process. Share your ideas, but be open to their suggestions and input. It is vital that the goal reflects what they care about, otherwise the project will not get the support it needs to succeed.

One useful check is that your planned improvement is aligned with the overall company strategy. A quick test to find out if you have got the right goal is to invite your sponsor and proposed team members to discuss this – if they don't have the energy or commitment to do so, then something is wrong: either the goal or your selection of the appropriate people.

Performance chart. This contains all the key elements that define your project and is the single most important item in the success report. Don't even think about skipping this section! The chart will show:

- The baseline data that you have collected on current performance.

- Mocked-up data to illustrate future performance (after improvements).

- The planned implementation start date. More details later, under 'Project plan: outline'.

Using the concept of 'make it real', this graphical depiction helps clarify what you are hoping to achieve and is an essential tool for ensuring alignment and getting others on board.

🎁 **Related special topic:** Using cycle time as a measure.

Success report Section 3: Project plan outline

The third section outlines how you plan to run the project. This includes target dates for milestones, the team members and agreed dates for key meetings. Here is an example from Sam's project:

3. Project plan outline

Milestones:

Team members:

Sponsor – Al Shah, UK head sales and marketing

Owner – Sam Goodman, head of UK customer service team

Team members:
- Leslie Jones, UK book order specialist (supplier)
- Sarah Franklin, northern region customer service team leader (process operator)
- Stephen Andrews, UK northern area customer services team (process operator)
- Susan Goodwin, UK fraud investigator (process operator)
- Nick Wiseman, online forum moderator (customer representative)
- Ash Pitman, data analyst (support)

Meeting dates:

Event	Date
Kick-off & Analyse meeting	4 Feb – full day
Design meeting	11 Feb – full day
Integration meeting	21 Feb – full day
Weekly meetings	Every Tuesday 10–11am from 28 Feb–27 June
Close-out meeting	4 July – 9–11am
Celebration event	7 July

Note that in the Success Cycle we are using standard milestones and timelines. These short timescales help to bring urgency and pragmatism to all projects. Remember less is more and that short timescales are the key to enabling rapid Iteration. You may be able to use even shorter timelines, but make sure you include all phases.

Standard milestones:

- **Draft success report.** The step of agreeing the draft success report is not a rubber-stamping exercise, it is a firm commitment from the key stakeholders to bring about the change and make the resources available to do so – in particular, people's time.

- **Implementation details.** Here you will have analysed your data, identified root causes and selected and designed solutions. You will also have developed an action plan to implement these solutions, including how you will monitor and measure the impact of the changes.

- **Change implemented.** To achieve this milestone, you will have done all of the things in your action plan, culminating in the launch of the improved process.

- **Final success report.** This is the point where you have *proved* the impact of the changes you have made and updated the success report with actual data. Crucially, you will have worked out a plan to ensure that the changes remain effective.

Team members. Once you have the project goal, then you can formally identify the team members who will actually conduct the project. In particular, the team needs to reflect, and be aligned to, the defined scope. As a minimum, the team needs to include representation of each of the groups involved in delivering the product or service, as well as a customer representative. A team of six to eight people works well. Note that if the project goal changes, the team membership may also need to be adjusted.

Meeting dates. Now you have the team identified, it is imperative to get project meeting dates booked with all members for the duration of the project.

You have four weeks to complete the Analyse & Design phase. The three key full-day meetings are:

- **Kick-off & Analyse.** This is where you explore and identify the root causes underlying the problem and establish team ways of working. Hold this meeting in the first week.

- **Design.** In this meeting, you will establish the improved process. Hold this meeting one week after the Kick-off & Analyse meeting.

- **Integration.** Here you define the plan for all of the work required prior to implementation of the new process. Hold this meeting one week after the Design meeting.

Key meetings for the remainder of the project:

- **Weekly meetings.** These are required throughout the phases for both Implement and Run & Learn. Booking these meetings now will help to avoid scheduling issues.

- **Close-out meeting.** This is the last of the weekly meetings and will need to be slightly longer. In it you will review the final results and what has been learnt.

- **Celebration event.** This is the point where you will have data proving that you have successfully improved the process. Note this is leveraging the 'power of the positive' – if you adopt the mindset that you are going to be successful, it becomes a self-fulfilling prophecy.

You have now drafted the first three sections of the success report. By investing this time and energy early on, you have vastly improved the probability of project success. There are two further sections in the success report which you and your team will complete later in the project, but first we have one more thing to attend to: contracts.

Contracts: team and sponsor

Another important part of alignment is contracting to clarify what the project expects of your team members and sponsor. You need to describe both their responsibilities and the resources you expect from them. By being specific, you are 'making it real' so that people properly understand what they are signing up for.

Here is an example team member contract from Sam's project:

Team member contract

Name: Leslie Jones, UK book order specialist

Project: Complaint Resolution Time

Role: Team member

Responsibilities: participate in all meetings; complete agreed actions between meetings; liaise with own department to keep people up to speed on the goal, timelines, impacts and progress.

Contracted time commitment:

Project phase	Agreed time commitment
Align	As required
Analyse & Design	Two weeks
Implement	One day/week
Run & Learn	One day/week

Each team member must be empowered to make decisions on behalf of the area that they represent. In particular, they will need to decide whether or not something will work in practice – and they need to have hands-on knowledge of the process to do this.

This does not mean that they can ignore the views of co-workers from their area – acting as a communication channel is definitely another of their responsibilities. As well as getting input from their area, team members are also responsible for reporting back on the progress of the team – their role as a communicator is two-way.

Be specific about the resource requirements that you need from your team members. Tell them how many days a week they will spend on team activities. This may be different for different phases of the project. Lay out the duration, frequency and dates of the meetings that you expect them attend – and put all of them in the calendar now.

You may not be sure how much resource you will need, so think of this the other way around. In the same way as you have set a fixed timescale for achieving the goal and the phases of the project and are working out what you can do by then to achieve it, set a fixed amount of resource that you expect from the team and then work back to define what you can all achieve with this.

Don't overlook your sponsor. The term 'sponsor' can have different meanings to different people, so meet with your sponsor to discuss their role and the help you are seeking.

Here is the example sponsor contract from Sam's project:

Sponsor contract

Name: Al Shah, UK head sales and marketing
Project: Complaint Resolution Time
Role: Team sponsor
Responsibilities: champion the goal of the project; agree resources for the project; assist in removing barriers to progress.

Contracted commitment:

Project phase	Agreed commitment
Align	Meet with project owner to help refine the documentation on current situation, destination and project plan.
Analyse & Design	Attend relevant sections of the following meetings: • Kick-off & Analyse • Integration
Implement	Attend regular meetings with project owner to provide help and support as requested.
Run & Learn	Attend review meetings with project owner to review data and consolidate learnings. Promote visibility of successes and learning. Attend team celebration.

Some of the standard things you will expect from your sponsor are to:

- **Champion the change.** Ask your sponsor to take every opportunity to speak positively about the change and educate others on what you are trying to achieve and why. This will help open up channels of communication and pave the way for a positive reception during implementation.

- **Provide resources.** Be clear on what you need and why. Often you will need the sponsor's help to get time commitment from key members on the project team.

- **Clear obstacles.** You and the team will be able to address most of the issues you encounter, but at times you may need a more senior perspective. Your sponsor is the first point of call for help in this situation.

Schedule regular review points with your sponsor. Again, put the dates in their calendar now. You can align standard meetings to the key milestones of the draft success report, implementation details and final success report. Provide your sponsor with an update at the milestone of 'Change implemented'. Of course, if you have issues along the way where you need your sponsor's help, meet with them wherever you are in the process.

Completion of the Align phase

Now that you have read through the first three sections in the draft success report, you might be wondering whether you really need to do all of this before you get started. Every few years, another book or research report comes out observing that the significant majority of projects fail (see Rowland and Higgs, 2008). Why is that? It is because the project team omitted or skimped on some/many of the elements of the success report we've just discussed. If you don't have these nailed down before you start, then the odds for success are stacked against you.

The purpose of the Align phase is to get agreement with key stakeholders on the navigation points for the project: Where are we going? Where are we now? What is the plan for the next iteration?

So do not proceed beyond this point until you have your target outputs:

SUCCESS REPORT (DRAFT)

1. **Current situation** ✔
2. **Project destination** ✔
3. **Project plan outline** ✔
4. Implementation details
5. Sustaining the change

CONTRACTS

Team members

Sponsors

It is hard to give a specific timeline for the Align phase, but if you are struggling to get agreement on your proposed goal, it is a clear sign that others don't see this as a priority. You then need to pause and reflect. If the Align phase takes more than six weeks, we suggest that you have open conversations to find out where the real problems lie.

Note that at this point, you are not trying to solve *anything*; you are not required to have *any* answers. At this stage, you are working out where you are going, putting fuel in the tank and deciding who will be getting in the car. Once you have established these few critical details, you are ready – so let's go! You now have everything you need to progress to the Analyse & Design phase.

Phase 2: Analyse & Design

Phases	Align	Analyse & Design	Implement	Run & Learn
Duration	< 6 weeks	4 weeks ★	6 weeks	12 weeks
Milestones	Draft Success Report	Implementation Details	Change Implemented	Final Success Report

In the Align phase, we collaborated with key stakeholders to set up navigation points for the journey ahead. We now have a shared understanding of where we are – the current situation, and where we want to get to – the project destination. We also have the critical details about how to complete the journey, as described in the project plan, all concisely documented in the draft success report.

The purpose of the Analyse & Design phase is to develop the implementation proposals. The ideas for implementation must be grounded in sound logical analysis and understanding of root causes, but we also aim to inspire the team to think differently about the challenge by engaging in the aspirational activity of defining the ideal.

The key **outputs** we need to develop during the Analyse & Design phase are documented in the draft success report under Section 4: Implementation details:

SUCCESS REPORT (DRAFT)

1. Current situation
2. Project destination
3. Project plan outline
4. **Implementation details** ✔
   - **Redesigned process** ✔
   - **Measures** ✔
   - **Action plan** ✔
5. Sustaining the change

The team creates the implementation details section of the draft success report over the next four weeks, primarily in the three full-day meetings that you have already scheduled. Some additional work will be required between the meetings.

The team must complete the Analyse & Design phase in a maximum of four weeks – time boxing this phase will ensure that the project can rapidly progress through this cycle of iteration so that you can quickly learn what really works. To achieve this, don't try to perfect everything; instead, work with your team and other stakeholders to iteratively develop your outputs so they are just good enough to get you to the next step.

Let's now work through the key meetings in turn, looking at the steps that the team takes in each.

Kick-off & Analyse meeting

The purpose of the Kick-off & Analyse meeting is to:

- Confirm with the team the project destination, milestones and current situation
- Agree team ways of working
- Discover and agree potential root causes

Where are we in the process? In the Analyse & Design phase, this is the first full team meeting and will take a whole day. Hold it within one week of gaining approval for the draft success report.

Here is the **meeting map**:

Prework	Agenda	Outputs
Team walk through process	1. Introduction	Agreed:
	2. Destination and milestones	• Destination
Meeting preparation	3. Ways of working	• Milestones
	4. Current situation	• Current situation
	5. Root causes	• Potential root causes
	6. AAR	

    Let's start by looking at the **prework**.

Team walk through process. If possible, the team goes to the workplace and follows a unit of work, for example a complaint, right through the process. Remember how listening in to customer complaint calls helped Sam's team really understand the customer's frustration at the delays? It also gave them insight into the hold-ups caused by waiting for order information and fraud checks.

Meeting preparation:

- Confirm sponsor is attending
- Create display items of the success report so far in a format useful for the meeting, eg enlarged printouts for the wall

 Let's now work through each of the **agenda** items in turn.

1. Introduction. This is about everyone getting to know each other. An icebreaker can help.

2. Destination and milestones. Ask the sponsor to headline their expectations of the team and then review the draft success report.

 Prior to this meeting, not everyone will have heard the same thing, so it is particularly important to establish a common understanding of the project goal. Being aligned on the Destination will serve as a foundation for the team to work together and make decisions going forward.

As team leader, make sure that everyone is clear on the following points illustrated by the chart in the draft success report.

Example: performance chart for Sam's project:

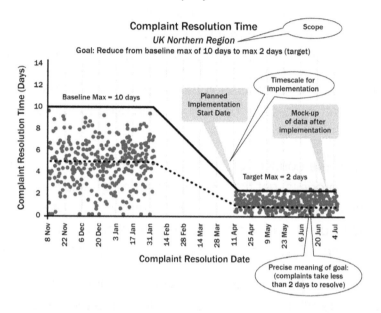

As well as being aligned around the project goal, ensure the team is clear about the project milestone dates.

Make sure everyone understands the timeline. The timeline is fixed and the team must buy into the concept of limiting what they do in the time available, rather than deciding what solution to implement and then working out how long it will take. This is a fantastic application of the concept 'less is more'. It may not be the way people are used to working, so spend time making sure they understand the concept. It is one of the most powerful tools you have for delivering success quickly.

3. Ways of working. This is a group discussion where the whole team defines their ways of working, meeting etiquette, and agrees their expectations of each other. It is good to set the tone as open and collaborative.

Of course, all teams run into issues as they progress. The important thing is to establish good ways of working from the outset, so that the team can quickly identify and resolve issues. This is true of team dynamics as well as technical issues.

4. Current situation. The team already has a draft process description annotated with issues in the draft success report, and you can use this to align the team during the meeting.

Using the concept of 'make it real' with a poster-size version of the draft process, get the team to walk through this and share their understanding. Let each person talk about how their group contributes and the issues they experience. Add sticky notes to further annotate the diagram with issues and concerns as these are discussed.

Remember, the goal of this exercise is to align everyone on the current situation and deepen understanding of the issues – not to create the perfect diagram.

5. Root causes. The discussion of the current situation will have prompted lots of engagement around the issues and the team will be keen to start fixing things, but rather than jumping straight into solutions, channel that energy into examination of the root cause of the issues. This step will ensure that you can create robust solutions which address what is actually causing the problem, rather than just trying to fix the symptoms you can see.

For example, in their Kick-off & Analyse meeting, Sam's team explored the root causes of long complaint resolution times. Using analysis tools (fishbone analysis and 5 Whys) to aid their understanding, they subsequently got a breakdown of the current cycle time, which confirmed their suspected root causes.

Related special topic: Analysing root causes.

The discussion in Sam's team suggested that the three main root causes were:

- **Incorrect address information** being entered by the customer on the original order form. The team suspected this to be the cause of many non-deliveries.

- **Lack of access to the order system.** When the complaints team want to check an address, they have to request it and wait, as this information is held in a system managed by the sales department.

- **Time-consuming fraud checks** run every single time a delivery complaint is made.

At this stage, it is important to consider what *additional* data you still need to collect to better understand root causes before starting to plan improvements. For example, Sam's team agreed that they needed to collect and analyse the following data to verify their root causes before the next meeting and assigned actions accordingly:

- Reasons for non-deliveries
- Cycle times for getting the order information
- Cycle time for fraud checks

6. AAR. At the end of the meeting, it is useful to reflect on how the team has been working together and what they have achieved. This will help embed the learning and provide momentum to continue trying new approaches.

📄 **Related tipsheet:** AAR.

Remember 'learn by doing' is a key concept within the principle of Iteration, so it is important to establish the regular practice of pausing and reflecting on how things are going.

You now have the **outputs** you need from the **Kick-off & Analyse meeting**.

 Meeting outputs:

Agreed:

- Destination
- Milestones
- Current situation
- Potential root causes

The team now has the clarity of purpose that comes from having a shared destination. They have been unified by the discussion and analysis about the root causes of poor performance. With these outputs, the team will be well prepared for the next stage and can confidently progress to the prework for the **Design meeting**.

Design meeting

The purpose of the Design meeting is to generate, evaluate and select a vital few improvement ideas for further development. These improvement ideas will be based on the detailed analysis of root causes and inspired by an understanding of the ideal situation, particularly from the customer's perspective.

Where are we in the process? In the Analyse & Design phase, the Design meeting is the second working meeting of the team. The meeting will take a whole day and should take place within one week of the Kick-off & Analyse meeting.

Here is the **meeting map**:

Prework	**Agenda**	**Outputs**
Collect and analyse data to confirm root causes.	1. Destination and milestones 2. Confirm potential root causes 3. Define ideal process and gap 4. Generate ideas 5. Evaluate and select ideas 6. Draft proposals (SDPs) 7. Allocate ownership of SDPs and actions to complete 8. AAR	• Ideal process • Outline proposals (SDPs)

Before the meeting, complete the following **prework**:

Collect and analyse data to confirm root causes. Before the meeting, collect any further data you require to pinpoint and verify root causes. The data you collect will, of course, be specific to your project and the root causes you have identified, but there are two key techniques that will be useful in many situations:

a. Cycle time analysis

b. Pareto analysis

Cycle time analysis is a simple but powerful technique which breaks down the overall cycle time into the sub-processes that are of interest. Using cycle time as your measure of success has several advantages, one of which is that it's an easy way to pinpoint the parts of the process that most contribute to the cycle time overall.

EXAMPLE:

Sam's team measures sub-process cycle times of fraud check and accessing order details:

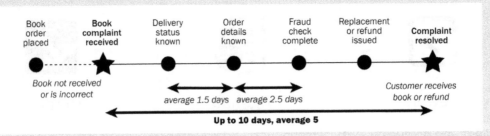

By looking at the breakdown of the overall cycle time for the different sub-processes, Sam's team could see that there were two major contributors: accessing order details, average 1.5 days, and completing fraud checks, average 2.5 days. Together, these two activities accounted for 4 of the 5 days of the average overall cycle time. This gave the team confidence that by addressing the root causes associated with these two steps, they could significantly improve the overall cycle time.

🎁 **Related special topic:** Using cycle time as a measure.

Pareto analysis is a powerful way of highlighting where to focus to get the maximum impact. Create a bar chart of your data, ranking the problems in order of frequency of occurrence, from highest to lowest. You will typically find that around 80% of the issue is caused by 20% of the problems.

EXAMPLE:

Sam's team created a Pareto chart on causes of non-deliveries for a sample of complaints:

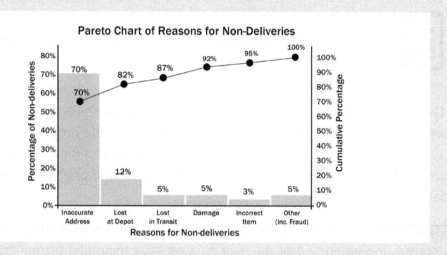

From this chart, they concluded that:

- Inaccurate address information was the highest-ranking cause of non-delivery (70%)

- Fraud was one of the lowest causes of non-delivery (<1%)

The last point was a particular surprise to the team as so much of the process time was spent investigating fraud.

 Related tipsheet: Pareto chart.

There are, of course, many useful tools to help you to analyse your process, but…

Beware! It is good to be aware of the risk of analysis paralysis. Remember you only need to study the current situation *until* you and the team have a common understanding of the potential root causes. Then move on. By collecting and analysing *sufficient* data to help you decide where to focus your efforts, you and your team can confidently move forward, knowing that you can make informed decisions about which solutions will be effective.

 Let's now work through each of the **Agenda** items in turn:

1. Destination and milestones. In the spirit of 'start at the end', it is always a good idea to briefly reiterate the goal and planned dates for the project. This simple step is amazingly powerful at keeping everyone aligned and focused. Don't forget to review the outputs and agenda in the meeting map and check that everyone is on board.

2. Confirm potential root causes. Update your process diagram with data that aids your understanding of the root causes – for example, a breakdown of cycle time or the results of Pareto analyses. Building a shared understanding means that you are well positioned to identify solutions which will address the real problem.

EXAMPLE:

Sam's team updated their process diagram with a summary of the information they had gathered about root causes:

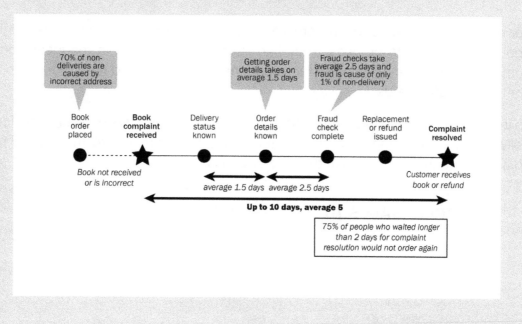

3. Define ideal process and gap. Until now, the team has been fully focused on understanding the reality of the current situation, but now you invite them to dare to dream and consider how things would be in an ideal world, particularly from the customer's perspective.

Ask the team:

- In an ideal world, how would this work?
- What would the ideal performance be?

In an ideal situation, the performance will be an extreme figure, for example, zero defects or 100% satisfaction. Remember this is an *ideal* so don't worry about whether or not it is achievable.

This is a great use of the Engagement concept 'power of the positive'. The purpose of defining the ideal is to stimulate new thinking, unconstrained by current expectations. It can feel liberating to have these discussions and will usually unleash great energy and debate.

For example, the discussion in Sam's team about the ideal led them to an insight about the complaints process. They had initially decided that in the ideal world, complaints would be resolved instantly and the customer would receive their book immediately afterwards.

As they were discussing this, one of the team said, 'Well ideally, we would have perfect deliveries and no complaints at all.' As a result, the team added the idea of no complaints to their definition of the ideal process.

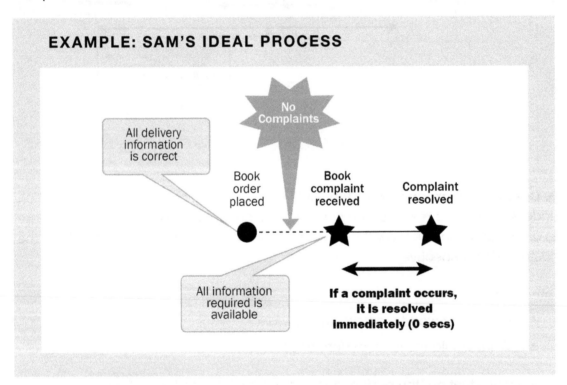

EXAMPLE: SAM'S IDEAL PROCESS

We can now quantify the size of the improvement opportunity, or 'gap'.

Gap = current performance – ideal performance.

For example, in Sam's case:

> The gap for the maximum time to resolve complaints = 10 days
>
> > Current max = 10; ideal = 0
>
> The gap for average number of complaints per week = 152 complaints
>
> > Current average = 152; ideal = 0

By defining the ideal process, you are making the long-term vision and the ultimate destination for the process real. The short-term destination for this project is made real through the output measure and target.

4. Generate ideas. Now is the time to build on the energy you've generated by discussing the ideal, and continue that creativity and lateral thinking to generate improvement ideas. Start by asking, 'How can we move towards the ideal?' and brainstorm ideas to close the gap and address the root causes.

Beware! Ensure that the team understands that they are *not* going to implement the ideal in one iteration. Often that would be extremely difficult and expensive. By looking at the process differently, and from the customer's perspective, you and your team can find cheap and quick ways to move *towards* what the customer wants.

Some of the basic rules of brainstorming:

- One idea per sticky note
- Put ideas up on a flipchart so that everyone can see them and build on each other's ideas
- Encourage the *whole* team to participate (go around the table, if necessary, to ensure one person doesn't dominate)
- No evaluation of ideas until the end
- Encourage laughter and outrageous suggestions – these often lead to great insights

It can be useful to use categories or headings to spark ideas for brainstorming. For example, you may wish to use your root causes as categories.

If you wish to reduce cycle time, three generic solutions can provide useful brainstorming categories:

- Reduce or eliminate waiting time
- Reduce or eliminate errors that cause rework
- Move steps off the critical path or do them in parallel

You will quickly generate a wall full of sticky notes capturing the team's thoughts. These can be consolidated and grouped to create a smaller set of unique ideas.

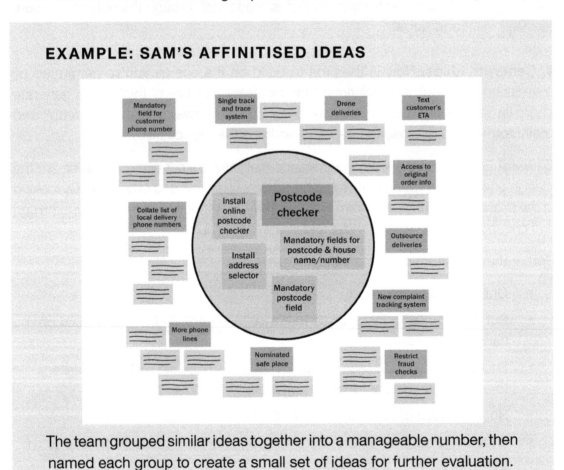

EXAMPLE: SAM'S AFFINITISED IDEAS

The team grouped similar ideas together into a manageable number, then named each group to create a small set of ideas for further evaluation.

5. Evaluate and select ideas. The next step is to identify the vital few ideas which will have high impact *and* can be implemented quickly. We recommend assessing each idea in terms of:

- **Time.** Can it be implemented by the agreed implementation date?
- **Impact.** How much impact will this have on the output measure? Use the data analysis you have already completed and/or compare pairs of ideas to identify those which will have the most impact.

By rigorously evaluating each idea against these two criteria, the team will be able to identify the vital few to develop further. An idea evaluation matrix is a useful framework to help make the decision clear. Draw the axes and lines indicating the cut-off criteria and plot each idea on the matrix.

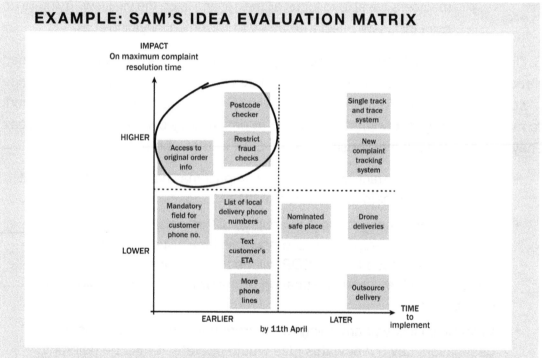

EXAMPLE: SAM'S IDEA EVALUATION MATRIX

Sam's team needed to decrease the maximum time to resolve complaints from 10 days to 2.

The target for 'time to implement' is the milestone from the outline plan in the draft success report. In Sam's case, this is 11 April.

[continued]

Based on this, the team selected the following three 'quick win' ideas to take forward:

1. Access to original order data

2. Postcode checker

3. Restrict fraud checks

Selecting a small number of impactful proposals that can be implemented within the time box is another way of leveraging the concept of less is more. This will pay dividends during the Implement phase when the team members are able to focus all their energies on the vital few. Trying to do extra things will affect their ability to implement anything at all.

6. Draft proposals (SDPs). The ideas that you have selected are currently defined through a heading and a handful of sticky notes, but this is not sufficient to provide a workable proposal. To further refine these, provide the team with a framework to make it real and show what is required to ensure they can implement the ideas. They can develop each proposal using an SDP format where:

- **Situation.** The current issues and what impact they have. Clarify the current situation with regard to this specific idea.

- **Destination.** What you want to achieve. Clearly state what the target outcome for this proposal is and how this idea will achieve the goal. Note, the destination for an SDP will be a more narrowly defined outcome compared to the overall destination of the project, but it should clearly contribute to it.

- **Proposal.** How you are going to get from your current situation to your destination. Lay out how this idea would operate. It may be helpful to develop a diagram showing how it interfaces with other aspects of the process. It will need a fully developed action plan (who, what, when) stating exactly how the idea will be implemented. Also include a proposal on how to measure if this improvement is working as expected.

Use this framework to develop the draft SDPs within the time available in the meeting. There will be a lot of unknown factors at this stage, so the SDPs need to include placeholders or working assumptions.

Example: one of Sam's team's draft SDPs:

Title	Provide access to original order information		
Owner	tbc		
Situation	Currently the operators who handle customer complaints are unable to access the full order information for a customer. They can only see the order numbers and items ordered, so if they suspect that the address information for that customer is incorrect, they must contact the sales department and wait for them to return the information. On average this takes 1.5 days. If the information is incorrect, they then email or call the sales department to have it corrected. This is a potential root cause of the complaint resolution taking so long.		
Destination	Provide direct access for the customer service team to the order delivery address information to reduce the time to access the delivery address down to 10 minutes. This will help reduce the overall time to resolve UK book delivery complaints (currently 5 days on average).		
Proposal	Design and implement an extract of the order database which is updated daily so that the complaints team has current addresses for each open order. Data will be extracted from the sales system and uploaded to a central database that is accessible to the complaint handlers.		

What	Who	When
Define a data extract for the order delivery information	Ash	29 March
Run a trial extract, check and adjust if necessary	IT/Ash	1 April
Train operators to use extracted data in central database to find address	Ash	7 April
Start using daily extracts	Complaints team	11 April

In-process measure:
- Time to make order details accessible – details for previous day's orders should be available by 8am

Related tipsheet: SDP.

7. Allocate ownership of SDPs and actions to complete. Each SDP will need some work to fill in the gaps, add detail and gain agreement from others to produce a fully developed proposal before the Integration meeting. The key first step in this process is to assign an owner for each SDP. These owners are responsible for the development of their SDP, but they will need help from others, both on the team and outside it. Ensure that they are super-clear about the actions required.

Example: Sam's list of SDPs and owners:

SDP title	Owner
Provide access to original order information	Ash
Limit fraud checks to orders over £200	Sue
Implement a postcode checker	Sarah

8. AAR. Just as with the Kick-off & Analyse meeting, reflect on what you've learnt and decide how you can improve your ways of working. Use the 'AAR' tipsheet to help structure your discussion. Don't be tempted to skip this step at the end of a long meeting; it's important to keep learning and improving.

You now have the outputs that you need from the Design meeting.

 Meeting outputs:

- Ideal process
- Outline proposals (SDPs)

The owners of the SDPs will already be invested in their solutions, so your role is to harness that momentum and ensure that they put flesh on the bones of the SDPs to develop well-rounded proposals to take forward into the Integration meeting.

Integration meeting

The purpose of this meeting is to consolidate the individual proposals selected in the Design meeting into a coherent overall action plan that will enable you to implement the new ways of working. The plan needs to include not only details of the changes, but also measures to evaluate the new ways of working.

Where are we in the process? In the Analyse & Design phase, the Integration meeting is the third working meeting of the team. The meeting will need a whole day and takes place within one week of the Design meeting.

Here is the **meeting map**:

Prework	**Agenda**	**Outputs**
SDPs	1. Destination and milestones 2. Review SDPs 3. Redesign the process 4. Review and define measures 5. Integrate the action plan 6. Sponsor review 7. Update draft success report 8. AAR	• Redesigned process • Measures and owners • Action plan

  Before the meeting, complete the following **prework**:

Develop SDPs. In the week between the Design and Integration meetings, you and your team need to do a lot of work to develop the SDPs. This is where all your upfront planning in getting people to clear their calendars will pay off as your team members will need some dedicated time to work out the details of their proposals, without distraction. As the team leader, it is your responsibility to engage with each SDP owner, not only to help them fine tune their SDP, but also to get an idea of how the proposals will fit together.

- Is it obvious how the current process will be changed?
- Are there any conflicting solutions?
- Is anyone going to be overloaded in implementing the SDPs?
- Do you need to secure any expert resource not already on the team?
- Will there be more than one change to a particular step in the process?
- Who will need training in the changes?

Although your team members have been picked because of their knowledge of the process, they will need to consult with others to develop the SDPs. Not only will this improve the quality of the SDPs, but it will also continue the process of wider engagement with stakeholders.

Let's now work through each of the **agenda** items in turn.

1. Destination and milestones.

Your team has been working on the detail of the SDPs and it is easy to lose track of what is important. Start the meeting by confirming the goal of the project and the timelines to focus the team on the destination. As usual, review the meeting outputs and agenda, and check that everyone is on board.

2. Review SDPs. Each SDP owner in turn leads a review of their SDP with the full team. Not everyone will have seen or given input to all of the SDPs so now is a good time to go through them together, so that everyone has the same level of understanding. They will also be able to see where there are common activities across the SDPs that can be co-ordinated, such as training.

As a team leader, ensure that you harness the power of the positive in these reviews and set the tone for others. This is particularly important since the SDP owners will now be invested in their proposals.

For example, Sam's team have selected the following improvements:

- **Postcode checker.** When the customer places their order, the system will look up the postcode to populate the address. This is to tackle the frequent problem of address information being inaccurate. The checker will reduce the number of incorrect deliveries, which in turn will reduce the number of complaints.

- **Daily listings of order details.** An automated process will be set up to provide a daily listing of the order information to the customer service team. This will mean they can immediately check address information, rather than having to wait 1.5 days for this information to be provided.

- **Limit fraud checks.** Fraud checks will *only* be conducted for orders over £200. Most orders are for less than £200, so this will mean that when they receive a complaint, the customer service team can immediately proceed with resolving the problem. Previously they had to wait on average 2.5 days for a fraud check to be completed. The further benefit is that fraud checks will now be processed in less than 1 day, as so few will be required.

3. Redesign the process. Start by working through your existing process diagram (from the draft success report) and annotate it with the changes that will result from each of the SDPs. Keep it simple, just enough detail to convey the essence of the changes you plan to make. Your solutions should include eliminating, redefining and/or rearranging some steps.

Then develop a strawman of the new process using the changes from the refined SDPs. Working on this together with your team, you will not only improve the quality of your strawman, but also engage the team so that they are all on board with how the new process will work.

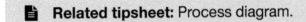 **Related tipsheet:** Process diagram.

Here's Sam's example:

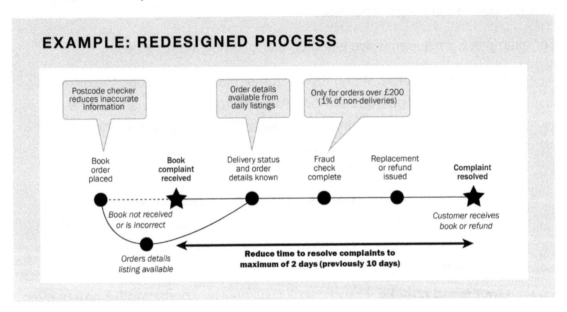

Consider how different your redesigned process looks compared to your original. A quick rule of thumb says that if it looks fairly similar, you may not have made adequate changes to make a significant difference to your output measure.

4. Review and define measures. While Sam's team already has an output measure of cycle time to resolve complaints to tell them whether they have been successful, they don't want to get to the end of the project to discover that the changes they have put in place aren't working as planned.

 Remember the concept of 'use evidence to make decisions'. Monitoring a small number of in-process measures will give the team an early warning system and enable them to take corrective action as necessary.

For all of the measures, both output and in-process, agree who owns them, ie who takes responsibility for ensuring they are collected, charted, reviewed and appropriately actioned. It is helpful to make it real and bring your measures to life by using mocked-up data, as Sam has done below.

EXAMPLE: MOCKED-UP IN-PROCESS MEASURE FOR SAM'S PROJECT

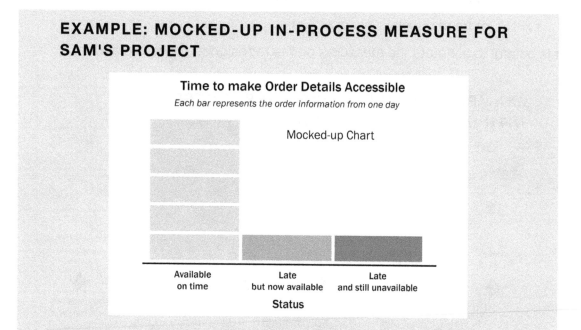

Time to make Order Details Accessible

Each bar represents the order information from one day

Mocked-up Chart

Available on time | Late but now available | Late and still unavailable

Status

This highly visual display is designed to alert Sam and her team when the new process is not working as expected. For days when the order information is late, a bar will be displayed in the appropriate column to indicate what action is required.

- Where the information is late and still not available, immediate action is required to find out and resolve whatever is holding it up

- For listings which were late but have now been provided, no immediate action is required, but the team will need to investigate to find out how to prevent this re-occurring

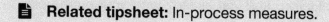

Related tipsheet: In-process measures.

All In-process measures for Sam's project:

- Time to make order details accessible. Owner = Ash.
- No. of complaints (overall). Owner = Sarah.
- No. of complaints due to incorrect postcode. Owner = Sarah.
- No. of fraud checks. Owner = Sue.

It is helpful to annotate the measures on the redesigned process diagram.

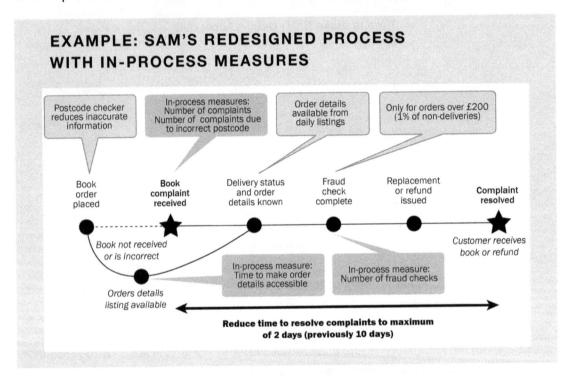

EXAMPLE: SAM'S REDESIGNED PROCESS WITH IN-PROCESS MEASURES

5. Integrate the action plan. You can now develop your integrated action plan. Don't even try to get into heavy duty project planning tools such as MS Project or similar. We have repeatedly found that *simple* plans that are visible to everyone and are regularly reviewed by the team are highly effective. And you already have your outline plan in the success report that shows your high-level milestones. In addition, all you need is a straightforward spreadsheet or table to document the detailed actions that need to take place. A key input to this exercise is a list of collated actions from the SDPs.

As well as the actions you need to take to implement each individual change, ensure that you include the following elements:

- What are the review steps?

- How are you going to measure the success of the individual changes? What data do you need to collect and who will review it and take action?

- Who needs to be trained, informed or otherwise engaged?

- Is there other 'infrastructure' that needs to be changed – systems, procedures, documentation etc?

The integrated action plan needs to specify *who* needs to do *what* and by *when*. This table will be the driver for your activities and the focal point of your review meetings during Implementation.

For example, here is the start of the action plan for Sam's project:

Action plan

Change Deliverable	What	Who	By when	Done?
Access to order information	Define a data extract for the order delivery information	Ash	29 March	No
Access to order information	Run a trial extract, check and adjust if necessary	IT/Ash	1 April	No
Access to order information	Train the teams	Ash/IT	7 April	No
Access to order information	Start daily extracts and record if received on time	Complaints team	11 April	No
Limit fraud checks	Gain finance approval to change	Sue	29 March	No
And so on				

The change deliverable column in Sam's table refers to the physical thing that is going to be delivered as a result of the proposals in the SDPs. It is useful to include this not only for tracking purposes, but also to make it real as to what will be delivered and what actions the team needs to take to complete delivery. Ensure your plan takes account of overlaps or opportunities for consolidation.

As with the redesigned process, further refinement and consolidation of the integrated action plan by the team will ensure their ongoing alignment and commitment to what they need to do.

 It is all too easy to focus just on the mechanics of implementation – what systems need to be changed, what listings need to be produced. But you must also 'seek to understand' the changes from the perspective of the people impacted – your customers and those who are responsible for running the process. This will help you identify the actions such as training and communication that need to be added to the plan.

6. Sponsor review. Ideally, bring your sponsor into the latter part of the meeting and walk them through the key points from your outputs: the redesigned process, in-process measures and action plan. Apply the concept of 'make it real' and display the outputs on flipcharts and sticky notes on the walls, rather than in a polished presentation. Your sponsor will feel more able to engage and give you specific comments, rather than just giving high-level feedback. Remember, the sponsor's role is one of overall guidance – for example, they may be aware of wider issues or opportunities that the team is not, so it is important to allow time for discussing these.

If your sponsor is not able to make the meeting, it is important to organise a meeting with them to complete this step and gain their endorsement.

7. Update draft success report. You can now update the implementation details section in the draft success report with the outputs of the Analyse & Design phase. If you are unable to do this in the meeting itself, ensure that it is completed immediately afterward.

8. AAR. You have now not only reached the end of the Integration meeting, you are also at the end of the Analyse & Design phase. Ensure that you reflect not only on this meeting, but also on the phase as a whole to capture the overall learnings of the team. Use the tipsheet: 'AAR' to help you structure your discussion.

You now have the **outputs** that you need from the **Integration meeting.** You will have agreed these outputs not only with your team, but also with your sponsor, and you will have updated the draft success report.

SUCCESS REPORT (DRAFT)

1. Current situation
2. Project destination
3. Project plan outline
4. **Implementation details** ✔
   - **Redesigned process** ✔
   - **Measures** ✔
   - **Action plan** ✔
5. Sustaining the change

Congratulations! You have reached the important milestone of completing the Implementation details. In calendar terms, the Analyse & Design phase is short, but it is intense.

All your hard work will pay off. The outputs your team has created will ensure that they are well prepared to start the Implement phase and put their plans into practice.

Phase 3: Implement

The Implement phase is the stage many people want to jump to as soon as they define the problem, but it is only now that you are ready to get going on building your solutions.

During the Analyse & Design phase, you and your team created the integrated action plan and got the sponsor fully on board and supporting your activities. The challenge during the Implement phase is to stay completely focused on executing the plan by the target date. This means completing all of the actions required to implement the new process and the in-process measures within the six-week timeframe.

The key **outputs** you are working towards in the Implement phase are:

Implement outputs:
- Completed actions
- New process launch

Implementation meetings

The simplest way to stay on track is to hold regular team meetings for the whole of the six-week period of the Implement phase. If you haven't already booked these meetings, get them scheduled now!

The purpose of the meetings in the Implement phase is to maintain focus and alignment among the team as they execute the action plan to ensure the change is implemented within the target six-week timeframe. Each meeting will have the same agenda focused on reviewing progress, resolving issues and learning.

Where are we in the process? These one-hour meetings take place every week during the Implement phase.

Implementation Meetings

Repeat x 6

Implementation Details   6 weeks   Change Implemented

Here is the **meeting map**:

Prework	**Agenda**	**Outputs**
Update action plan	1. Destination and milestones 2. Review action plan 3. Manage issues 4. AAR	• Updated plan • Actions to resolve issues • Learnings

 Before the meeting, complete the following **prework**:

Update action plan. Ask the owner of each set of actions to update this prior to the meeting.

 Let's now work through each of the **agenda** items in turn:

1. Destination and milestones. Briefly reiterate the goal and planned dates. It may seem repetitive to do this in every meeting, but your team members may be working on several different things and this quick reminder keeps everyone focused.

Also, review the outputs and agenda for this meeting and check everyone is on board.

2. Review action plan. Ask the owner to lead the review of actions for their area. Bearing in mind the 'power of the positive', set the tone and start on a positive note by briefly mentioning what has gone well and/or recently been completed. The main discussion needs to focus on anything which has issues.

Example: here's an extract of the action plan from Sam's team. In it you can see that the team found an issue with part of the design and had to divert resource to help fix it.

Change deliverable	What	Who	By when	Done?	Issues/ opportunities
Provide access to original order details	Define data extract for the order delivery details	Ash	29 March	Yes	
Provide access to original order details	Run a trial extract, check and adjust if necessary	IT/Ash	1 April	No	Extract so far is slow, Ash to help IT investigate by 4 April
Provide access to original order details	Start daily extracts and record time to find the details	Operators	11 April	No	
Limit fraud checks to orders over £200	Gain Finance approval to change	Sue	29 March	Yes	
And so on...					

Plans can and do change. For example, prototyping with customers will uncover issues and opportunities, and you will need to change actions as a result. As your plan iterates, keep reviewing it and evaluate any changes in terms of their impact on the goal. Make sure that you and the team stay on track to implement the first set of improvements by the target date.

3. Manage issues. The purpose of this discussion is to capture and address any *new* issues which might impact the project plan. It's really important to encourage your team to raise issues and opportunities so you can make sure you are on track, so:

- Thank those who raise issues and make sure it is a positive experience for them

- Focus on what needs to be done to bring you back on track and record the agreed actions

- Make sure decisions are recorded so that they will not need to be revisited

It's vital to your success to communicate with, and get feedback from, people *not* in the core team. You may need them to complete some of the actions in the action plan, and you will need them to support the changes once they are operational, so their buy-in to what you are doing is crucial. If the team picks up concerns, they need to highlight these at the weekly meetings, where the whole team can be involved in assessing the impact and resolving issues.

4. AAR. Include a short but meaningful discussion at the end of every meeting to fuel ongoing improvement in the team's ways of working.

- Ensure there is genuine discussion about what is working well for the team and where things could be improved.

- Follow the standard approach to AARs to make sure you are recording and assigning actions to implement learnings as you progress. See the tipsheet: 'AAR'.

You now have the **outputs** that you need from this Implementation meeting.

Meeting outputs:

- Updated plan
- Actions to resolve issues
- Learnings

Additionally, the team will feel reconnected and energised by the shared sense of purpose and progress. Most importantly, people will know what they need to do over the coming week to make sure the project stays on track.

By methodically repeating the Implementation team meeting each week, you will steadily progress towards the point where the change can be implemented. This simple agenda enables you to have the right conversations at the right time to ensure that the whole team remains focused on rapidly delivering the change.

Use time boxing to manage Implementation

To stay on track, use time boxing for the implementation activities.

To help focus meeting discussions:

- Implementation meetings should not take more than one hour
- Have fixed agenda timings
- Make sure that you stick to the allotted time

The same holds true for the overall goal. You have a fixed end date by which to achieve this – six weeks from having agreed the implementation details.

- Stay committed to the original timeline. This will help the team to stay focused.

- If you find out that you can't do what you had planned, change the plan, not the end goal. If you can't rejig your plan, reduce your scope rather than extend your end date. For example, apply the changes to less work.

When Sam's team realised they couldn't implement a postcode checker in time, they came up with the idea of making the postcode field mandatory which they could achieve in the timescale.

With this approach, you will still achieve implementation, gain a real business benefit and have all the knowledge that you need to go on and make further improvements in subsequent iterations.

Completion of the Implement phase

You now have the following outputs:

Implement outputs:

- Completed actions
- New process launch

The final meeting of this phase confirms that all actions have been completed: all of the changes and in-process measures have been implemented and are now operational.

With all of the change deliverables in place, the team can congratulate themselves. They have reached a major milestone of 'Change implemented'. Don't forget to send an update to the sponsor to let them know your team has reached this important milestone and to confirm that you are still on track to deliver measurable change by the agreed date.

In Sam's team, the completion of the Implement phase meant that they had successfully implemented three key ideas to improve the process. And they had done this by 11 April, the agreed date for the milestone of 'Change implemented'. It took a huge amount of self-discipline to keep it all time-boxed and focused on the Destination.

Here's exactly what Sam's team implemented:

Changes implemented
Provide access to original order information Limit fraud checks to orders over £200 Postcode and house number/name mandatory
In-process measures implemented
Time to make order details accessible. Owner = Ash. No. of complaints (overall). Owner = Sarah. No. of complaints due to incorrect postcode. Owner = Sarah. No. of fraud checks. Owner = Sue.

The key success factor in the Implement phase is making sure that everyone is fully aware of progress and actions required, and understands their responsibilities for resolving any issues. The team needs to work closely together to make sure this all happens smoothly, so keeping everyone engaged and informed through the implementation meetings is vital.

As the team moves into the next phase, Run & Learn, their focus will shift from implementing actions to monitoring the changes and reviewing feedback – including measures and data. They will focus their actions on what to adjust, rather than what to create. This is a vital learning phase for the team.

Phase 4: Run & Learn

The improved process is now up and running, so customers will be starting to benefit from the changes you and the team have made. The Run & Learn phase is all about understanding the impact of the changes, consolidating what you have learnt and making sure that the changes are sustained. Indeed, this is an opportunity to consolidate *all* of the learning you've gained throughout the project and make sure that it is synthesised into an actionable plan. This will ensure the long-term success of the change, once the first cycle of iteration is complete.

The key **output** you are working towards is the full and final success report:

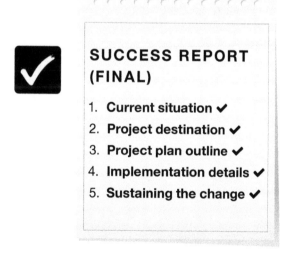

To finalise the success report, you need to update several key elements, particularly the performance chart to show actual data and any further revisions to the process and measures. Finally, you need to enter details in Section 5, Sustaining the change, to capture your learnings and define how you and the team will sustain the improvements.

The Run & Learn phase is the perfect opportunity to apply the Iteration concepts of 'learn by doing' and 'use evidence to make decisions'. You have up to twelve weeks to conduct the Run & Learn phase, which is specifically designed to allow sufficient time to gather robust data to properly evaluate how the new process is performing.

It is vital to success to allow adequate time to collect sufficient data to demonstrate that the team has achieved a sustained change. Dependent on the details of your measure, you may be able to do this in fewer than twelve weeks, but make sure that you allow sufficient time and are not simply reporting an initial spurious positive result.

The weekly team meetings you held during the Implement phase need to continue as Run & Learn meetings. The final team meeting, held at the end of the Run & Learn phase, is called the close-out meeting. This is the culmination of all your hard work, as you will finally have sufficient data to properly evaluate the impact of your changes and can complete the success report.

Related tipsheet: Performance chart.

Run & Learn team meetings

The purpose of the meetings in the Run & Learn phase is to maximise the probability of success by closely monitoring how the new process is running and taking action where appropriate. Each meeting will have the same agenda focused on reviewing measures and feedback, resolving issues and learning.

Where are we in the process? Weekly team meetings are held throughout the Run & Learn phase, where the process is being monitored and data collected.

Here is the **meeting map**:

Prework

Measures and feedback

Agenda

1. Destination and milestones
2. Review measures
3. Review feedback
4. AAR

Outputs

- Actions to resolve issues
- Learnings

 Before the meeting, complete the following **prework**:

Collect data on measures and feedback. This phase is driven by data so it is essential to collect the following information:

- Data on the in-process and output measures

- Feedback from customers and process workers

 Let's now work through each of the **agenda** items in turn:

1. Destination and milestones. Briefly reiterate the goal and planned dates. Review the meeting outputs and agenda to check that everyone is on board.

2. Review measures. Start by reviewing each of the in-process measures. In the early days of running the new process, the in-process measures are likely to be the most helpful and illuminating. Remember the concept 'use evidence to make decisions'. You've set up the in-process measures to provide alerts if the new process is not running as intended, so it is important for the owner of each one to watch the data closely and be ready to jump into action to address deviations.

EXAMPLE OF AN IN-PROCESS MEASURE CHART FROM SAM'S PROJECT:

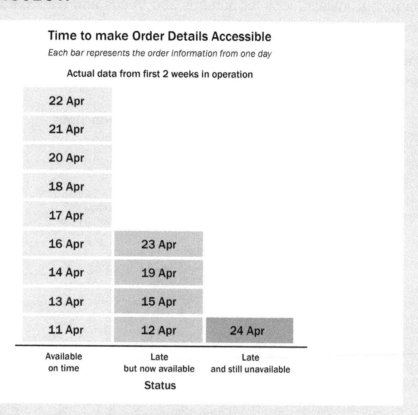

Time to make Order Details Accessible

Each bar represents the order information from one day

Actual data from first 2 weeks in operation

Available on time	Late but now available	Late and still unavailable
22 Apr		
21 Apr		
20 Apr		
18 Apr		
17 Apr		
16 Apr	23 Apr	
14 Apr	19 Apr	
13 Apr	15 Apr	
11 Apr	12 Apr	24 Apr

Status

Using this type of highly visual display alerts Sam and her team when the process is not working as expected. For days when the order information is late, a bar is displayed in the appropriate column to indicate what action is required.

On 24 April, the information was late and is still not available. Sam is now taking immediate action to identify and resolve the problem.

On the 12, 15, 19 and 23 April, the listings were late but have now been provided, so no immediate action is required. But Sam and her team are going to investigate to find out how to prevent this re-occurring.

📄 **Related tipsheet:** In-process measures.

As data becomes available for the primary output measure, plot this on the performance chart and review it at each meeting. It is important not to react to individual data points; instead, look for patterns and trends and work out what the causes of these are.

Sam's performance chart shows some long cycle times following initial implementation of the improved process.

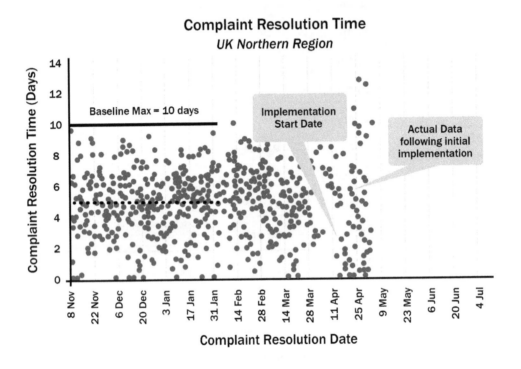

Do not despair if this happens to your process, it is very common. With all your focus and energy on the process, it is likely that some difficult cases which have been trapped in the system for a long time finally got resolved, and this is a cause for celebration! Keep going and the subsequent data will illustrate that the new process really has made a dramatic improvement.

3. Review feedback from customers and process workers and define any corrective action you may need to take.

As you run the new process, you have the potential to get a lot of feedback quickly as everyone will be keen to let you know what they think. It is important to have established lines of communication so that you can hear what the customer and the people working in the process are saying. Remember to use the concept 'seek to understand' and really listen to people. It may well be that a few simple tweaks could make all the difference.

4. AAR. Follow the standard approach to AARs at the end of every meeting to make sure you are recording and assigning actions to implement learnings as the project progresses.

You now have the **outputs** that you need from this Run & Learn meeting.

Meeting outputs:

- Actions to resolve issues
- Learnings

Again, the team will feel reconnected and energised by the shared sense of purpose and progress, and will know what they need to do over the coming week to make sure the project stays on track.

The Run & Learn meetings continue until the penultimate week of this phase. Then you conclude the project with the final team meeting: the close-out meeting.

The close-out meeting

The primary purpose of this meeting is to ensure that the improvements will be sustained in the future through an effective project closure and handover. Additionally, it is important to consolidate what the team has achieved and learnt, so that they and others can build on this experience in the future.

Where are we in the process? This is the final meeting of the team and is held in the last week of the project.

Note this is *not* a one-hour meeting. Allow at least two hours. It is important that all team members attend, and it can be rewarding to have the team sponsor attend at least some of the meeting so that the team can hear, directly, their reflections on what has been achieved.

Here is the **meeting map**:

Prework

Measures

Feedback

Learning

Identify process
owner

Agenda

1. Agenda and milestones
2. Review performance chart
3. Confirm new process and measures
4. Confirm process owner
5. Agree closing actions
6. AAR

Outputs

- Updated chart
- Confirmed:
  - » New process
  - » Measures
- Process owner
- Close-out actions
- Learnings
- Final success report

 Before the meeting, complete the following **prework**:

- **Collect data on measures**
  - » Collect data on the output measures
  - » Collect data on the in-process measures

- **Collect feedback**
  - » Collect customer feedback
  - » Collect process worker feedback

- **Reflect on learnings**
  - » Ask team members to reflect on the whole project so they can bring their individual learnings to the meeting

- **Identify process owner**
    - » Liaise with the sponsor to establish who will be the process owner going forward. There may need to be some further discussions to finalise this.

It is really good to meet with your sponsor before the close-out meeting to update them on the results of the change and brief them on the sort of comments you are hoping they will make at the meeting. This includes recognition of the results, appreciation of the *way* the team has worked together and the rigorous approach that has been taken. In these early days of developing new ways of working, recognition from a senior figure will make a huge difference to how the team approaches the *next* project.

 Let's now work through each of the **agenda** items in turn:

1. Agenda and milestones

- Remind the team of the purpose of the meeting and review the agenda

- Remind the team of the timelines you have been working to

2. Review performance chart. Now the team can finally look at the full data, all feedback and the updated performance chart. The following review questions help evaluate the impact the changes have made:

- What do the results tell you?
- To what extent have you achieved the target you set at the beginning?

EXAMPLE: PERFORMANCE CHART FOR SAM'S PROJECT

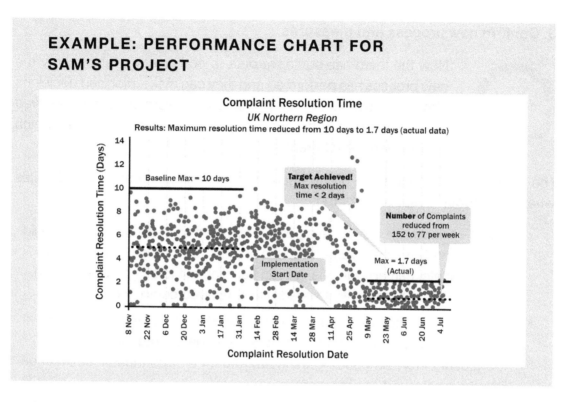

Complaint Resolution Time
UK Northern Region
Results: Maximum resolution time reduced from 10 days to 1.7 days (actual data)

Start by quantifying the improvement in the output measure, as defined by the team at the outset. For example, in Sam's project the complaint resolution time had fallen dramatically from a maximum of 10 days to just 1.7 days. Using the concept 'define measurable goals' really pays off as you come towards the end of the project and have hard data to illustrate what your team has achieved.

The improvement needs a fanfare of recognition. Well done to the team! They have exceeded their target. Note that this magnitude of improvement is normal for teams who run their projects according to the principles outlined in this book.

Note also the significant spin-off bonus. In Sam's project, in addition to reducing complaint resolution time, the changes also radically reduced the actual number of complaints received by the customer service team from 152 per week down to 77. This was largely driven by the adoption of the mandatory postcode field, which helped to significantly reduce the number of problems occurring in the first place. Eliminating issues at source is always the best type of solution.

3. Confirm new process and measures

Now the team has sufficient data to confidently evaluate how the new process has performed and they can make informed decisions about how to proceed. For example, some elements of the improved process will clearly be beneficial, but there may be others which make little or no difference.

The team works through each of the changes they've implemented and decides whether to adopt, adapt or abandon:

- Adopt = the change has made a positive contribution to the result and should be confirmed and consolidated into the process, eg through training, documentation etc. Perhaps the change can be rolled out to other areas. If it can, how should this happen? Who needs to be involved/convinced?

- Adapt = the change may require some tweaking to make it work better. If this is the case, you will need to do more experimentation and collect more data before embedding the adaptation. Perhaps these ideas can go into the next round of improvements.

- Abandon = the change did not make a difference to the result or made the results worse than before. In this case, reverse out the change from the process and record what you have learnt. If one of your changes has not been beneficial, the likelihood is that a factor that you *thought* would have an influence on the result has not, so you may rule out changes to that factor in the future.

The success report may need to be updated with a revised process diagram of the improved process, if anything has changed since you updated it in the Analyse & Design phase. Additionally, the team needs to check the in-process measures and make any adjustments to ensure they still reflect the key elements of the improved process.

Sam's team chose to implement just *three* key improvements which they monitored through in-process measures. Let's look at how these improvements are performing:

Root cause	Solution	Current performance
Lack of access to the order system. When the operators want to check an address, they have to request it and wait, as this information is held in a system managed by the sales department.	Provide a daily listing of order details to the customer service team.	The process of providing a listing of order details to the customer service team is now working smoothly. The list is provided within one day of the order being placed, which means the team has immediate access to address information if/when a customer makes a complaint.
Time-consuming fraud checks are run every single time a delivery complaint is made.	Limit fraud checks to orders over £200.	The number of fraud checks being conducted has been reduced from an average of 30 per day down to just 1 per day. Checks now take less than 1 day to complete, as so few are required.
Incorrect address information being entered by the customer on the original order form.	Make entry of the postcode mandatory.	The number of complaints caused by the address being incorrect has reduced from 95 per week to 15.

Update the process diagram and definition of in-process measures to reflect the team's final decisions.

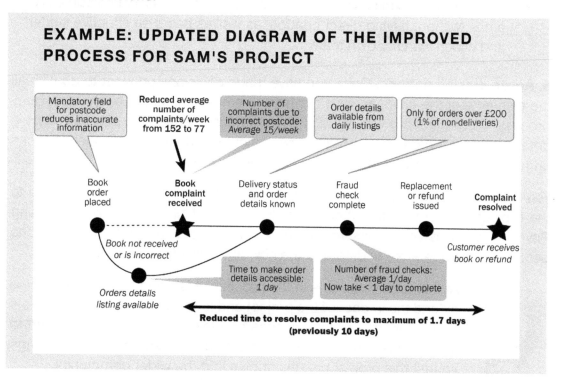

4. Confirm process owner. As part of the prework for this meeting, you will have met with the sponsor to identify who the long-term process owner will be. If you selected the right team members at the start, it is probably now obvious who has long-term ownership for the areas that have changed. Update the success report with the name of the process owner.

> *Long-term process owner for Sam's project:*
>
> Sarah Franklin, northern region customer service team leader

Sarah was chosen because:

- She brought great energy and enthusiasm to the project and quickly grasped the improvement concepts
- She is clearly ready for further career progression and will embrace the opportunity to become a role model and really drive for further improvement in the process
- She is quick to form positive working relationships across multi-disciplinary areas (without having direct control), as well as being an effective leader and coach with her own team

5. Agree closing actions. Once you have made decisions on what to do with all the elements of the change, work out how to embed the change into the overall process. Closing actions will include things like documenting the process steps in detail so that all operators can learn how it should work and future operators can understand how and why the process operates as it does.

You may also need to do formal training of people who have not been close to the project. The project team members may be best placed to run the training. Planning for this is vital to ensure the process does not revert to how it was done before and the operators understand the how and why of the changes.

At this reflective stage in the process, it is good to consider how to extend the impact of the project and identify who else might benefit from sharing your experiences and learnings. Prompt the team to agree some actions to publicise the success and the team learnings, so that this project creates ripples into the wider community.

It is often useful to pose the following specific questions:

Where else could we apply this process? For example, Sam's project was scoped for the northern region, but she has already been talking to one of her team who runs the southern region customer service team. They have expressed strong interest in what Sam and her team have achieved.

How might we further improve this process? Sam's project implemented one solution which gave the customer service team daily listings for the original orders, but there may be a better way to do this in the longer term. Now that the team has data proving how important this is, it may be worth exploring other solutions.

Summarise all this in the success report. Note that you now need to hand management of this action plan over to the long-term process owner, who has ongoing responsibility for managing these actions to completion.

Closing actions for Sam's project:

What	Who	By when	Done?
Deliver presentation at next sales meeting to showcase our improvement and how we achieved it.	Sam	5 July	Yes
Update all documentation associated with the new process to reflect the changes.	Leslie	18 July	No
Design and run training for agency operators (who provide holiday cover).	Nick	25 July	No
Meet with southern region customer service team to share our learnings and kick start next project.	Sarah	18 July	No
Meet with IT to explore possibility of providing operators with direct access to order information (instead of daily updates).	Ash	31 July	No
Etc.			

6. AAR. This is a big opportunity for you and the team to apply the concept of 'learn by doing' and reflect on what you've learnt about the process of making improvements. Record these observations and plans in the success report as it will be valuable for others in the company to learn from your experience. Sam's team found that although some of the ideas for improvement were specific to their project, there were a lot that could be used on different initiatives in the future.

Example: here are some of the team learnings for Sam's project:

Learnings (extract):

What went well?

- The root cause analysis really helped us to understand what was going on with the process
- Sam kept on reminding us of the timelines – it meant we never lost focus on the end date

What could be improved?

- When we were working on the SDPs we didn't always get input from our departments. Getting buy-in was easier if we did this and we had more confidence in our proposals.

Actions (extract):

Who?	What?	When?
Sam	Work with southern region customer service team and sponsor to ensure future projects use team contracts to establish team member responsibilities for getting input	31 Aug

You now have the **outputs** that you need from the close-out meeting.

Meeting outputs:
- Updated chart
- Confirmed
  - » New process
  - » Measures
- Process owner
- Close-out actions
- Learnings
- Final success report

At this point you have completed all of the elements of the project and documented these in the final success report. Once the team members are satisfied with this, share the document with the project sponsor – not only to gain their endorsement and recognition of the change, but also to show how you have achieved it.

To see the final document for Sam's project, go to the next section in Part 2.

Celebrate your success

A key element in ensuring people remain motivated is to recognise their effort and success.

By applying the 'power of the positive', you will have a celebration booked in the calendar already.

Finding a suitable way of celebrating the team's success is crucial to recognition. It could be a party, a physical memento of the project, or the opportunity to present the project to a wider/more senior audience. A personal recognition – for example a heartfelt thank you or public acknowledgement from a sponsor or customer – is often much more appreciated than an anonymous addition to a payslip.

Completion of the Run & Learn phase

You have now completed all project activities and have the final output: the full success report:

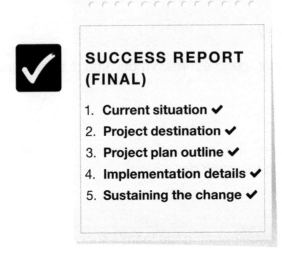

SUCCESS REPORT (FINAL)

1. **Current situation** ✔
2. **Project destination** ✔
3. **Project plan outline** ✔
4. **Implementation details** ✔
5. **Sustaining the change** ✔

The key outputs of the Run & Learn phase are the plans for sustaining the change in the future, as documented in the final success report. It is vital to have ownership established to carry forward the new process and the learnings. Additionally, having the final success report documenting the actual results you've achieved is a critical input for the next iteration of improvement.

By this point, you may well be feeling both elated *and* exhausted. Making real improvement takes grit, determination and a lot of hard work. Congratulations! You have fully engaged your team in completing one full cycle of improvement and moved closer to the destination. You will almost certainly be closer to the ideal than you were previously, and subsequent iterations will take you even closer.

Sam's Final Success Report

Here is Sam's full and final success report.

Complaint Resolution Time Success Report

1. Current situation

Customers' problem:

UK customers have been experiencing difficulty with deliveries. Issues related to book deliveries account for 62% of the complaints to the UK customer service team. Furthermore, these customers wait up to 10 days for complaints to be resolved, with an average of 5 days to resolution. This is reducing repeat business and potentially driving down sales.

Current process:

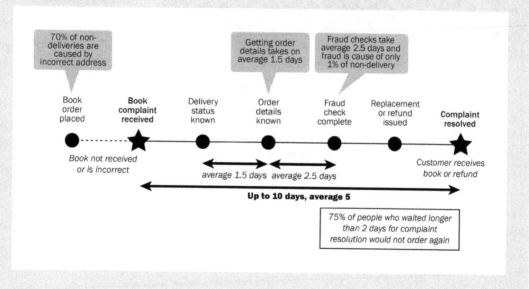

2. Project destination

Goal statement:

Reduce complaint resolution time for the northern region from a maximum of 10 days to a maximum of 2 days by 4 July.

Performance chart:

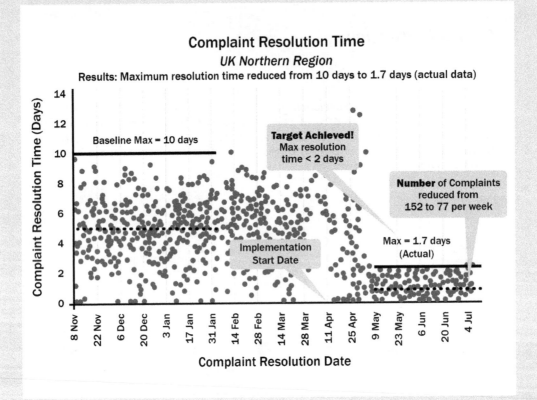

3. Project plan outline

Milestones:

Team members:

Sponsor – Al Shah, UK head sales and marketing
Owner – Sam Goodman, head of UK customer service team

Team members:

- Leslie Jones, UK book order specialist (supplier)
- Sarah Franklin, northern region customer service team leader (process operator)
- Stephen Andrews, UK northern area customer services team (process operator)
- Susan Goodwin, UK fraud investigator (process operator)
- Nick Wiseman, online forum moderator (customer representative)
- Ash Pitman, data analyst (support)

Meeting dates:

Event	Date
Kick-off & Analyse meeting	4 Feb – full day
Design meeting	11 Feb – full day
Integration meeting	21 Feb – full day
Weekly meetings	Every Tuesday 10–11am from 28 Feb–27 June
Close-out meeting	4 July – 9–11am
Celebration event	7 July

4. Implementation details

New process:

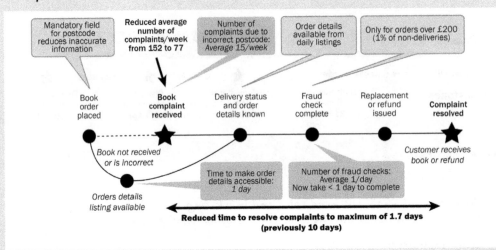

In-process measures:

In-process measures implemented:
- Time to access order information. Owner = Ash
- No. of complaints (overall). Owner = Sarah
- No. of complaints due to incorrect postcode. Owner = Sarah
- No. of fraud checks. Owner = Sue

Action plan:

Change Deliverable	What	Who	By when	Done?
Access to order details	Define data extract for the order delivery details	Ash	29 March	Yes
Access to order details	Run a trial extract, check and adjust if necessary	IT/Ash	1 April	Yes
Access to order details	Start daily extracts and record time to find the details	Complaints team	11 April	Yes
Limit fraud checks to orders over £200	Gain finance approval to change	Sue	29 March	Yes
And so on				

5. Sustaining the change

Process owner:

Sarah Franklin, northern region, customer service team leader

Learnings (extract):

What went well?

- The root cause analysis really helped us to understand what was going on with the process
- Sam kept on reminding us of the timelines — it meant we never lost focus on the end date

What could be improved?

- When we were working on the SDPs we didn't always get input from our departments. Getting buy-in was easier if we did this and we had more confidence in our proposals.

Actions (extract):

Who?	What?	When?
Sarah	Meet with southern region customer service team to share our learnings and kick start next project	18 July
Sam	Work with southern region customer service team and sponsor to ensure future projects use team contracts to establish team member responsibilities for getting input	31 Aug
Sam	Deliver presentation at next sales meeting to showcase our improvement and how we achieved it	5 July
Ash	Meet with IT to explore direct access to order details	31 July

Sustaining Success User Guide

Once you have implemented a change using the Success Cycle, the challenge is to make sure that the change sticks.

In Step 3 in Part 1, we followed up on Sam's project to illustrate how to apply the success principles to sustain the initial success. This section provides more detailed guidance on how to make this happen for your change. We will review how to run process review meetings, as this is the engine that powers sustaining improvement. We will also go through establishing process ownership and defining the next set of improvements.

To ensure that you maintain and enhance the success you have achieved, you require three key things:

- Process ownership
- Process review meetings
- Further draft success reports

Process ownership

One of the key steps in the Run & Learn phase was to appoint a process owner. Now we need to ensure that they fully understand what the role entails.

The role of the process owner is vital to sustaining the change. They are responsible for managing the performance of the process as a service to the customers and championing future improvements. This includes:

- Monitoring the ongoing measures
- Reviewing the results with customers on a regular basis
- Identifying issues and potential improvements

It is also vital that the team operating the process is involved in ownership of the process and its performance. This team needs to continue to evolve the destination and move towards it. This may mean keeping certain aspects of the current performance stable while improving other aspects.

EXAMPLE

In Sam's team, Sarah takes on the role of process owner. She sets up regular review meetings with the process team. In the initial meeting, she delegates responsibility for each of the measures. Each measure owner manages the data collection and leads the review of the latest data in the regular meetings. Sarah takes personal responsibility for gathering and reviewing the customer feedback.

Sarah also engages with customers and senior managers who have a stake in the process and validates that reducing complaints is now a key aspect of their destination.

Process review meetings

The purpose of these meetings is simple: to proactively manage the performance of your process to meet customer needs over the long-term. They also serve to maintain the focus and momentum of the team of people now running the process on a day-to-day basis.

When?	Dependent on the turnaround speed of the process, this might be ten minutes every day, half an hour once a week or one hour every month, but it needs to be absolutely set in stone that it always happens with the prescribed frequency. This is one meeting that you never cancel. Set them up now for the rest of the year. Expect that regular attendees will arrange for deputies to provide cover, when required.
Who?	The process owner will probably lead these meetings. Attendance also needs to include key people such as those running each specific aspect of the process. It is great if possible to include suppliers and customers as well. If not, then set up separate meetings with these groups to engage them and review their feedback.
How?	Make the meetings real by having a standard agenda and keep discussions focused via time boxing. A great way to do this is to have a stand-up meeting around a dashboard. This displays the relevant measures in conjunction with an action plan. Record the amendments to the actions as you go.

A dashboard summarising the metrics will make them easily visible to the participants and provide a framework for the meeting. Each metric has an entry on the dashboard with a summary of performance and whether or not it is on target. This makes it quick and easy to identify where the discussion needs to be focused.

As well as the quantitative measures, it is also informative to collect qualitative information – eg customer feedback on how well they feel the process is performing. Mismatches will require discussion and are a fruitful source of insight.

Where are we in the process?

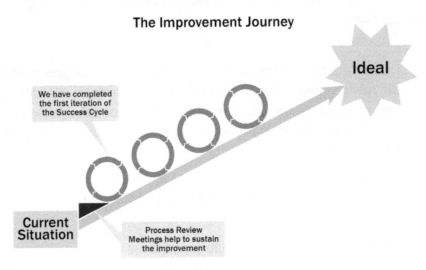

The Improvement Journey

Here is the **meeting map**:

Prework

Gather:

- Output and in-process measures
- Customer and process worker feedback
- Action plan

Agenda

1. Hot news
2. Review dashboard
   - Output measures
   - Customer feedback
   - In-process measures
   - Actions
3. AAR

Outputs

- Updated action plan
- Learnings from the meeting

Before the meeting, complete the following **prework**:

- **Collect data**
  - » Collect data on the output measures and update the charts
  - » Collect data on the in-process measures and update the charts

- **Collect feedback**
  - » Collect customer feedback
  - » Collect process worker feedback

- **Update actions**
  - » Ask the owners of any actions to update the action plan prior to the meeting

Let's now work through each of the **Agenda** items in turn:

1. Hot news. Ask the team to share one or two recent good news items. These can be small achievements; a learning from something which has gone wrong; an opportunistic discussion in a lift that led to an important insight. This is not a competition about who has achieved the most since the last meeting; it is about nurturing a sense of learning together, collaborating and having fun. This agenda item needs to be time-boxed carefully so as not to impinge on the remainder of the meeting.

This is a great use of the Engagement concept 'power of the positive'. The review of successes starts the meeting on a positive note. Encourage laughter and a relaxed atmosphere. The unspoken message is that this is a team that works well together, gets things done and is constantly seeking new opportunities to improve.

2. Review dashboard. Reviewing your information in a dashboard format makes it quick and easy to identify the areas of concern and focus the conversation accordingly.

For example, Sarah and her team set up a permanent dashboard on a wall near their coffee area, where they gather for their meeting. The team can refer to this at any time. It consists of the status and latest chart for each measure, customer feedback and actions associated with each.

Example – part of Sarah's dashboard:

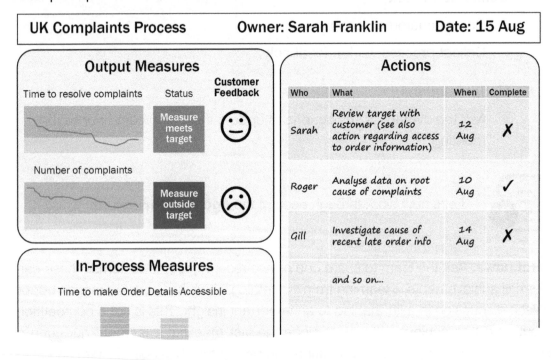

📄 **Related tipsheet:** Dashboard.

The tone of the discussions about the information contained in the dashboard is important. Where something has been marked as 'outside of target', frame the discussion in positive terms, for example 'Let's understand what has led to this. What do we need to do to protect the customer? How do we prevent this from happening again?' The unspoken message is 'How do we work together as one aligned unit in service of our customer?'; the atmosphere is of mutual respect and appreciation. If anyone starts to apportion blame, quickly turn the discussion back to how to move forward. You may need to explicitly state that this is how the team is going to work.

Let's look at the different types of information on the dashboard.

Output measures. These give you information on how well the process as a whole is meeting the customer's need. For output measures, it is useful to indicate the customer's target on the measure chart. In Sarah's example, the different zones on the chart indicate whether the data point is on or outside of target. This makes it easy to determine whether or not the process is currently on target or not – Sarah has explicitly called this out next to the chart.

🎁 **Related special topic:** Collecting and reporting data.

Beware! Just as one swallow doesn't make a summer, one data point in the target zone doesn't prove that you have established a permanent change. Expect measures in a stable process to fluctuate around an average – if one data point happens to fall within the target zone on your chart, it doesn't necessarily mean that the next one will follow suit. A good rule of thumb is that you can only claim you are meeting a target if at least seven consecutive data points are within the target zone. Process variation is a great topic for further exploration – one book that might help you is *Understanding Variation: The key to managing chaos* by Donald J Wheeler.

Focus the discussion of the output measures around the customer's needs, whether the process is meeting them, and what positive actions you and the team need to take.

Customer feedback. Your metrics and measures provide quantifiable information to help you focus on improving performance. But only looking at the data won't give you the full picture – for this you need to talk to your customers on an ongoing basis.

How do your customers feel about the performance of the process and the service that you provide to them? A quick temperature check – for example asking your customer to assess your process as red, amber or green – is a good starting place to focus your conversation.

The output measures are tremendously powerful in this ongoing customer dialogue: does the data accurately reflect their experience? Is this what really matters to them or do the measures need fine tuning? Have you met the original target, and if so, what is their next priority? Having this data may well point you to new areas for future improvement.

It's not uncommon for your customer to give a different assessment to the quantitative one that you've determined from your agreed measures and targets – you might think everything is OK and their temperature check is red! Look deeper to find out why – perhaps there is an emerging issue that is not covered by your measures, or their priorities have changed. You may need to adjust the measures that you use as a result.

Follow the same principles for these discussions with your customers as for your data review – set the example of treating all concerns as positive opportunities for improvement.

In-process measures. While the output measures reflect the overall performance of the process in relation to the needs of the customer, the in-process measures reveal the performance of key sub-processes.

Monitoring the in-process measures will give you an early warning system to flag where things might not be working as intended. The key to these measures is to use them on an ongoing basis to proactively take action to bring the process back on track, as shown in this graphic.

EXAMPLE: ONE OF THE IN-PROCESS MEASURES FOR SAM'S PROJECT

Time to make Order Details Accessible

Each bar represents the order information from one day

Actual data from last 2 weeks in operation

17 Aug		
16 Aug		
15 Aug	22 Aug	24 Aug
14 Aug	20 Aug	23 Aug
13 Aug	18 Aug	21 Aug
11 Aug	12 Aug	19 Aug

Available on time	Late but now available	Late and still unavailable

Status

The chart makes it clear that the operators are often not receiving access to original order information within the target timescale – there are lots of bars on the chart in the 'Late' categories. Sarah has assigned an action to investigate the root cause.

As well as immediate actions to bring individual items back on track, you may also need longer term actions to investigate and fix root causes leading to process failure.

Actions. After the review of all the information on the dashboard, the next step is to review and update the actions accordingly. Additionally, if there are any non-complete items for which there are concerns, also review these items. The discussion is about a) understanding what the problem is, and b) defining what the team can do to bring the item to completion. Assume that everyone is trying their best, so if there is a problem, the team as a whole needs to work together to resolve this.

3. AAR. Once the dashboard review is complete, a quick AAR helps ensure that the real conversation happens. What are the issues that are not getting raised? How do people feel about the meetings? How well is the team working together? See tipsheet 'AAR'.

You now have the **outputs** that you need from this process review meeting.

Meeting outputs:

- Updated action plan
- Learnings from the meeting

By regularly holding these meetings, you will proactively work towards meeting the needs of your customer. Not only will your customers be happier, but there will be beneficial effects for your team too as they learn and develop.

Establish support mechanisms. For the regular review meetings to thrive and do their job of sustaining and improving process performance, they need ongoing support mechanisms to deal with issues that the team cannot resolve directly. Predefining both who and how this will operate will make it much easier. The *who* means having a long-term sponsor, or perhaps a wider steering group that you regularly update on progress. The *how* is an escalation process defining how the team will be engaged.

You may need to coach the sponsor or steering team so that their interventions are always appropriate and to ensure they don't meddle. The important thing here is not to undermine the process owner or their team. They have absolute responsibility for the day-to-day running and management of the process.

Further draft success reports

The last component in sustaining success is to start the next iteration of improvements.

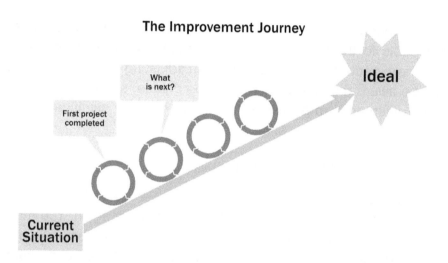

This means choosing some more short-term goals that will drive you towards your ideal and building on the success you have already achieved. In practice, this means starting another iteration of the Success Cycle by creating new draft success reports. There are two main types of improvement to consider: applying the change you have already made to a wider scope, and determining new ways to accelerate towards the ideal.

Extending the scope

Is it possible to extend the changes you have made to encompass a wider scope? You may have defined this when completing the sustaining success section of the success report, or you may decide this is possible when reviewing customer feedback. This will be much more straightforward than the first iteration of your improvement cycle as you now know what changes you need to make and what results you can expect. The destination here is much easier to define and justify as you already know what you can achieve, but there are two things to consider before rushing headlong into this.

Firstly, engage if you want to go faster. The new scope may include different process operators, different customers of the process and different suppliers, perhaps a different sponsor. If so, go back to the Align phase and engage these people in the new scope. Take along members of your current team who can help to influence and answer questions and concerns people may have.

Secondly, collaborate with the new people involved to identify if there are any different aspects to the new scope that may have an impact on the proposed changes or the expected result. This may mean adjusting your implementation plan to suit, but be aware that everyone likes to be unique, so be ready to objectively evaluate any differences to assess if they are sufficiently significant to warrant a change in approach.

Further iterations towards the ideal

Consider the question 'What other changes can we make to get closer to our ideal?' This will mean iterating around the Success Cycle again. You may be able to do this more rapidly now that you have some experience and feel more confident in applying the principles, concepts and tools we have been sharing. Also, your team will have learnt more about the factors that influence the performance of the process and have evidence to back it up.

Where to focus your efforts for the next Success Cycle will depend on how close you are to your customer's ideal, and how important achieving that ideal is to your customer. While you should continually monitor and manage your process, you will need to identify the vital few areas where iterating through further success cycles will make the most difference.

By engaging in the activities described in this User Guide, you will have established:

- Process ownership
- Process review meetings
- Further draft success reports

Taken together, these three things will ensure you maintain and enhance your initial success and that customer satisfaction continues to grow.

Tipsheets

After Action Review (AAR)

What is it?	An AAR is a dedicated discussion focused on identifying learnings, based on an activity that has just taken place, eg a meeting or a project. The discussion includes identifying what has gone well and what could be improved. The outcome will be a short set of actions based on the learnings.
Why use it?	The purpose of the AAR is to ensure that the team actively reviews what happened and what they can learn, and agrees what is useful to take forward. It is a key tool to support the concept of 'learn by doing'. Regular AARs also help with engagement as people feel more involved and energised by identifying and implementing better ways of working.
When?	Use AARs at the end of every meeting throughout the Success Cycle. Generally useful after any meeting. Also useful at the end of specific phases and at the conclusion of any piece of work.
How?	An AAR should include everyone who was involved in the original activity.

Pitfalls	• Leaving the AAR for too long after the work has been completed. It is really important to conduct the AAR right after the meeting/project has finished so that everyone can remember exactly what happened. • Many teams make the mistake of only conducting an AAR at the *end* of a large piece of work. This deprives the team of the opportunity to 'learn by doing' and apply their learnings *throughout* their work together. • Sometimes AARs can degenerate into a blame game. It is important to keep the focus on learning. Learning is an inherently positive thing. It doesn't matter how well or how badly things have gone, everyone *can* do better next time. • Not identifying or implementing actions based on what you've learnt. These actions should be taken seriously to embed the learning. • Keeping important learnings just within the team. Spread the word about what you have learnt and the whole company benefits. • It is easy to overlook the learning opportunity from things that have gone well. Consider how you can apply successes elsewhere.

Note: AAR is a popular technique used in a variety of forms, eg benefits and concerns. Whichever way you choose to use it, the important thing is to do it frequently and act upon it.

Dashboard

What is it?	A graphical representation of the performance of a process and the status of activities being carried out to improve it.
Why use it?	The purpose of a dashboard is to increase engagement by making the process performance real to people. This enables a team to see the vital few areas where they need to focus their efforts to make a difference to the customer.
When?	Generally create it after the first iteration of process improvement and use it continuously thereafter. It is useful for both steady state operation and during subsequent improvement projects.
How?	Create a wall-mounted or electronic dashboard with the following content. 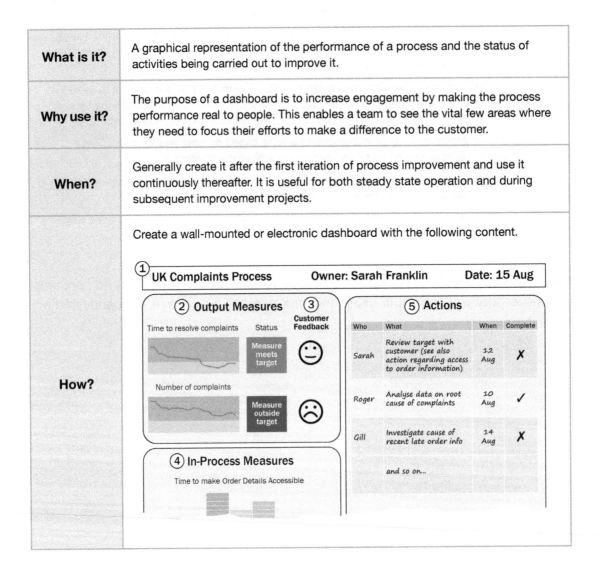

How *[continued]*	1	The title of the dashboard identifies the process, the owner and when it was last updated.
	2	Graphs of the output measures show the current performance of the process and whether or not it is meeting the agreed customer need.
	3	Include some form of customer feedback. This may be actual data, comments or a representation of the latest feedback.
	4	Charts show performance of the in-process measures, highlighting potential problem areas in the process.
	5	A list of actions, the owners, target completion dates and status show what the team is doing to make improvements or address issues.
	Review the measures, customer feedback and actions at the process review meetings.	
Pitfalls	• If you don't actively maintain the data and it becomes out of date, the team will soon consider the dashboard irrelevant and lose interest. • If the team fails to regularly review the dashboard and action list, then any effort to maintain the data will be pointless.	

Related tipsheets: Performance chart; In-process measures.

Related special topic: Collecting and reporting data.

Defining your customer

What is it?	Your customer is the person or group who benefit from the things that you do.
Why use it?	By ensuring that your product or service meets your customers' needs, you can ensure that your efforts are worthwhile. 'Do what matters to your customer' is one of the key concepts within Destination.
When?	You define your destination and your customer during the Align phase of the Success Cycle.
How?	1. Identify the output of your process – what is the product or service that your process produces? For example: resolved complaints, reports, website designs, packaged goods. 2. Identify the groups who **directly** receive these products/services. They could be outside or inside of your company. These are your **primary customers**. 3. Where your product/service is used internally, identify the **ultimate customer** outside the company. The ultimate customer is the last person/ group who receives the benefit of your product/service. For example, a clinical study report is used to determine whether a drug is safe and effective, and is delivered to internal customers and a regulatory authority. The ultimate customer is the patient who receives the drug. Design your process to meet the needs of your primary customers. Then evaluate the impact on the ultimate customer as a check step in your decision making.
Pitfalls	• Your customer is usually a group of people. You may have different processes and outputs for different customer groups – for example, you may design websites for both internal and external customers. Don't get distracted by the differences – aggregate your customers where the high-level processes and issues are similar.

Pitfalls *[continued]*	• Similarly, you may have a whole chain of customers who benefit from your product/services. For example, the goods you have packaged may pass through many different distributors and retailers before finding their way to the ultimate customer. If each of the elements of these chains focuses on the primary and ultimate customers' needs, they will work seamlessly. Don't be distracted by all the different parts of the chain. • For purely internal processes (for example, expense processing), the ultimate customer outside the company will not receive a direct benefit. The benefit to them will be that you are not diverting resources from the products/services that they receive, so the process needs to be done efficiently.

In-process measures

What is it?	In-process measures provide a real-time alert when a key step fails to comply with the standard process.
Why use it?	The purpose of in-process measures is to enable you to take timely corrective action so that you still achieve your intended outcome, even when something has gone wrong. If it is not possible to completely correct things, the alert should enable you to manage expectations and/or take steps to protect the customer. In-process measures are a practical application of the concepts 'learn by doing' and 'use evidence to make decisions' as they provide real-time feedback on how your improved process is actually running in practice.
When?	In-process measures are particularly relevant in the Analyse & Design, Implement and Run & Learn phases of the Success Cycle. It is key to set up the in-process measures before you start running the new process to provide immediate feedback. Learnings from the feedback may indicate further work is required and/or adjustments to the process.
How?	1. Ask the question 'To achieve the performance goal, what are the critical success factors (CSFs)?' 2. For each CSF, set up an in-process measure to track how well you comply with the intended process and provide an alert when you need to take action. 3. Define the process for reviewing and responding to the data. For example, in Sam's process, one CSF is that the original order information needs to be available to the complaints team by 8am the following morning. Sam's team set up an in-process measure to record whether the information was available on time for each day. This enabled them to take appropriate and timely action.

How *[continued]*	**Time to make Order Details Accessible** *Each bar represents the order information from one day* **Actual data from last 2 weeks in operation**

Time to make Order Details Accessible

Each bar represents the order information from one day

Actual data from last 2 weeks in operation

Available on time	Late but now available	Late and still unavailable
17 Aug		
16 Aug		
15 Aug	22 Aug	24 Aug
14 Aug	20 Aug	23 Aug
13 Aug	18 Aug	21 Aug
11 Aug	12 Aug	19 Aug

Status

Pitfalls

People often define the measure in such a way that it only provides retrospective information. To take *proactive* corrective action:

- The information has to be available real-time
- The data has to be looked at frequently
- The alert needs to be visible and unambiguous

Meeting maps

What is it?	A meeting map is a structured approach to ensure meetings are effective and efficient. The meeting map defines the destination (the meeting output) and the plan to get there (the agenda and prework).
Why use it?	A meeting map is a practical application of the Destination principle, in particular the concept of 'start at the end'. By getting upfront alignment on the meeting destination, you can be specific about what the agenda should look like to achieve this and the prework you require, including making sure you have the right people attending. This leads to: • Shorter, more focused discussions • Quicker, better decisions • Enjoyable and productive meetings as people are more engaged
When?	All meetings benefit from having a meeting map. Even impromptu meetings can be started by defining the destination, ie target outcomes.
How?	It really is as easy as 1-2-3: 1. Start by identifying the destination, ie the required meeting outputs. Then work out the plan to get there. 2. Design the agenda with timings to deliver the stated outputs. 3. Define the prework you need so that you can complete the agenda in the meeting. Example meeting map:

Prework

Agenda

Outputs

Background data
on problem X

Draft proposal

1. Introduction (5 mins)
2. Review data (10 mins)
3. Review and finalise proposal (15 mins)
4. Action plan (10 mins)
5. AAR (10 mins)

Agreed
proposal

Actions

Pitfalls	• It is easy to make the mistake of assuming everyone is aligned on the target outcomes. Pre-circulate the meeting map to all participants so everyone knows what to expect and how they can contribute. Start the meeting by checking if any changes are needed to the meeting outputs. • It can be tempting to over-discuss items. Propose realistic timings on the agenda and keep to these. • If one person does all the preparation, others may be quite disengaged coming into the discussion. It works better to share out the meeting preparation, then everyone arrives feeling engaged and prepared.

Note: The meeting map is based on the Input-Process-Output (I-P-O) technique, resolving a common confusion on where to start by explicitly applying 'start at the end' with the outputs.

Paraphrasing

What is it?	Paraphrasing is a process of concisely summarising what you have heard after intensely listening to others.
Why use it?	Paraphrasing is an essential tool to deepen engagement and particularly supports the concept of 'seek to understand'. Often in discussions, we are not really listening to each other; we are just waiting for a pause in the conversation so that we can make our own points. The purpose of paraphrasing is to: • Clarify what you've heard to avoid misunderstanding • Conduct better quality conversations through respectful appreciation of the perspective and ideas of others
When?	This is helpful in all stages of the Success Cycle and in all discussions. It is particularly helpful: • At the start of a project when you want to really understand the experience and concerns of others • If someone is expressing concerns and/or behaving obstructively • If you are finding it difficult to get your point across, ask others to paraphrase what they heard you say
How?	**Listen** Give the speaker your complete attention **Summarise** what you heard **Check** for understanding. Ask the speaker if your summary correctly captured the main points **EXAMPLE** When you hear a customer express concerns or issues, concisely repeat them back in your own words. You might say something along the lines of, 'Let me check I have understood correctly. I think I heard you say that the product we provide to you has had problems in each of the last three consignments, and although you were still able to use it, it has taken a lot of time and effort from your staff to deal with the situation. Is that correct?'

Pitfalls	• Don't let the speaker talk for too long without summarising what you heard, otherwise it will be hard to capture the essence of their points. • People sometimes repeat *everything* that was said. It is more effective if you *summarise* what you heard. This is a skill which improves with practice. • People sometimes jump to conclusions without first checking with the speaker that their summary was correct.

Pareto chart (or analysis)

What is it?	Pareto analysis is a simple technique to help identify the most common sources of an issue, eg non-deliveries. It is a key tool to support the concepts of 'use evidence to make decisions' and 'less is more'. Also known as the 80:20 rule, it is a way of using data to investigate your theories about the root causes of a problem.
Why use it?	The purpose of a Pareto chart is to highlight the most important among a (typically large) set of factors. For example, use it to represent the most common sources of defects, the highest occurring type of defect, or the most frequent reasons for customer complaints, and so on. We use Pareto analysis so that we can target our improvement efforts on the vital few areas which will have the most impact.
When?	It is used in the: • Align phase to define project scope. For example, it might be that 80% of the issues occur in one or two geographical regions. • Analyse & Design phase to verify your root causes. It can also be useful for some in-process measures for reporting on the process dashboard.
How?	1. Identify the problem you want to investigate, eg complaints, defects, returns. 2. Decide on your problem categories and collect frequency data for these categories. 3. List the categories with their count data in decreasing order of frequency. See example table below. 4. For each category, calculate the percentage of the total and the cumulative percentage. The final cumulative percentage should be 100%. 5. Create a bar chart of the count data showing the '% of total' on the left-hand axis. 6. Plot a line of the cumulative percentages, referencing the right-hand axis. 7. Identify the top few causes, cumulating to roughly 80%. These are the *vital few* to focus on to achieve the most benefit.

EXAMPLE: Sam's frequency table

Reasons for non-delivery	# Occurrences	% of total	Cumulative percentage
Inaccurate address info	9,200	70%	70%
Lost at depot	1,574	12%	82%
Lost in transit	679	5%	87%
Damage	605	5%	92%
Incorrect item	428	3%	95%
Other (including fraud)	650	5%	100%
Total	**13,136**	**100%**	

How [continued]

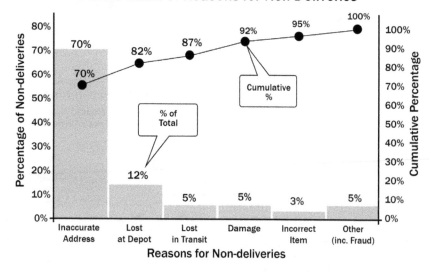

Pareto Chart of Reasons for Non-Deliveries

Pitfalls

- If you have even sized bars on the graph, either you don't have enough data or you have made an unsuitable choice of categories.

- A category of 'other' that falls in the top two or three rankings. There is an important root cause hiding in this category, so you need to investigate what types of things fall into 'other'.

- Not using enough data – you need a lot of data points for this to give you good results, say 100 data points minimum.

Note: most spreadsheet software will automatically rank the data and create the graph for you. Type 'Pareto' into the help function for instructions.

Performance chart

What is it?	A performance chart is a graphical depiction of the performance of a process over time.
Why use it?	The purpose of a performance chart is to show if, and how, the performance varies over time, including any trends, patterns and shifts, particularly with reference to targets.
When?	At all stages of the Success Cycle as well as over the long term. The purpose will change from defining the initial problem to demonstrating performance changes over time.
How?	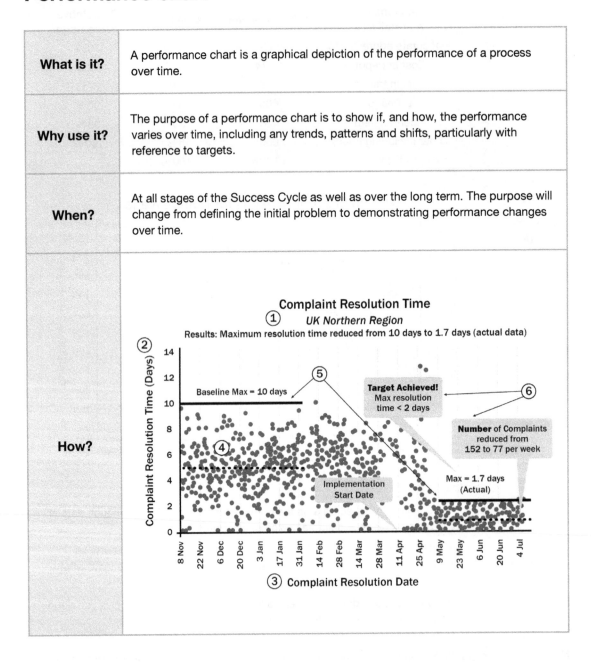

How *[continued]*	**1**	The title of the report primarily identifies the measure which is being displayed. Additional information may include: • The scope for the project, eg UK northern region • A summary of the performance of the process and any sustained changes
	2	The vertical axis is the output measure – the indicator that will demonstrate how well the process is meeting your customers' needs.
	3	The horizontal axis is time – this shows data from before the project was started through to the end of the project. This allows you to see changes and trends.
	4	Plot each individual datapoint on the two axes. By doing this, you can see what is really happening. For example, you may see that when you started implementation, there were a few long cycle times as the backlog was cleared, and after the implementation of the changes, there are consistently fewer complaints. Note that in this chart, all the data is actual data. You use mocked-up data in the draft success report to make the target change real for the team.
	5	Summary statistics (maximum and mean) are just that – an overall summary of the performance. These values are used in the title of the chart.
	6	Annotate key features of the data and what they mean. Here, the change is the most important feature, so this is the most prominent annotation. Highlighting the implementation date makes it easy to evaluate the difference between before and after.
Pitfalls		• Summary statistics (mean, maximum) don't replace the full data picture. Ensure you plot all the data wherever possible. • **Beware** of celebrating too early! One data point is not proof of a change. Rule of thumb: look for at least seven consecutive data points within the target zone.

Process diagram

What is it?	A process diagram is a visual depiction of the key features of a process, including measures.
Why use it?	The purpose of creating a process diagram is to: • Focus the team on the few key things that affect the performance of the output measure • Align the team so that they have a common understanding and direction
When?	In each phase of the Success Cycle, use the process diagram to focus/align people on what is important, eg: • In the Analyse & Design phase: illustrate root causes of the issues, the proposed solutions and in-process measures • At the end of the Run & Learn Phase: show how well those solutions have worked and the results from the in-process and output measures
How?	Take a single landscape page of paper/slide/flipchart.

1	Start at the end – what is the output that you deliver to your customer? Put a description of this on the right-hand side of the page.
2	Define the step which triggers the start of the process to create the stated output. Put a description of this towards the left-hand side of the page. Precede it with any key inputs.

How *[continued]*	3	Fill in the process steps: what are the few key steps that turn the inputs into the outputs? Add these to the page and join the steps together to indicate the flow through the process. It can be useful to add an operational definition of key steps (*in italics on process diagram*).
	4	Add the current data that you have on to the diagram. For cycle time, indicate where the measurement starts and ends.
	5	Use callouts to annotate issues/root causes/solutions, depending on where you are in the improvement cycle.
Pitfalls		• Using more than one page/six process steps will dilute the team's focus. • Don't do it on your own – create a process diagram as a team or as a strawman for discussion. • Don't define your output as what matters to the process operator. Focus on the customer by using 'complaint resolved' not 'complaint closed' (they may be quite different). • Similarly, don't just define activities; specify the completion status of each step (eg complaint received, refund issued).

Situation-Destination-Proposal (SDP)

What is it?	An SDP is a problem-solving framework used to create a proposal. SDP stands for the three key elements in the framework: situation, destination, proposal.
Why use it?	The purpose of an SDP is to create a robust proposal that explicitly addresses the issues with the current situation to achieve a clearly specified destination.
When?	The SDP framework can be used for any problem with a short-term goal and limited scope. Within the improvement cycle, SDPs are used in the Analyse & Design phase to define and develop the proposals selected by the team.
How?	For your problem, define: **Situation** – the current issues and what impact they have on the customer. **Destination** – what you want to achieve through implementing the proposal. Define a measurable goal. **Proposal** – how you are going to get from your current situation to your destination. • What you plan to implement. Make your proposal as real as possible – perhaps mock up what you are proposing to implement and/or describe how it will work. Include when the proposal will come into effect and what pieces of work will change. • How – an action plan (who, what, when) stating exactly how the idea will be implemented. Don't forget to include engagement activities, especially for those whose ways of working will change, and collection of measures to demonstrate the proposal is working. **EXAMPLE** Situation: 85% of team meetings in the last month overran. A small survey showed that attendees are unclear about what team meetings are trying to achieve so find it difficult to make decisions, resulting in long discussions. Destination: reduce percentage of team meetings that overrun in the next month to <25%. Proposal: for all meetings from 1 June, the chair will distribute a meeting map containing outputs, agenda (with timings) and prework 2 days before the meeting.

	Who	What	When
How *[continued]*	Jo	Review mock-up of meeting map with team	At next meeting
	Al	Create meeting map template for team use	By 20 May
	Bim	Work with team to create meeting map for the first meeting and distribute to attendees	By 28 May
	Jo	Identify team meetings in June and work with Bim to coach the chairs in use of meeting maps	By 1 June
	Al	Ask the chairs to collect data on meeting timings	By 1 June
Pitfalls	• Don't describe what the situation is *not* – say what it *is*. • Ensure that the destination is a goal that could be addressed by different proposals (and *not* the inverse of the situation). • Avoid vague words like 'complex', 'unreliable' and 'simple'. Be definitive and spell out how something is demonstrably having an impact. Where possible, use data to show this.		

Note: SDP is an extension and adaptation of the S-T-P technique created by Fred Fosmire.

Help, I'm Stuck

The Success Equation is wonderfully simple so hopefully you will find it effective and easy to remember, but if you are feeling a bit daunted and are thinking that your problem is different, you are not alone. Over the years we have heard many arguments that a more complicated model is needed and responded to countless cries for help.

Whenever you feel stuck, go back and refer to the principles and concepts of the Success Equation.

We know that these principles and the concepts underlying them work in practice – they have proven themselves to us time and time again in many different circumstances. And whenever something hasn't gone well, we can always trace it back to a point where the principles haven't been applied effectively. So when you face a problem, think about how you can apply the principles to what you are facing. By doing this for yourself, you will 'learn by doing' and build up your own resource of experience.

To help you on your way and illustrate what we mean, here are some common sticky situations that people face, with corresponding ideas on how to address these using the Success Equation principles and concepts.

Problem	Solution
We know what we need to do – it is a waste of time to worry about defining specific goals and collecting data.	Let's consider the challenges if you don't have a clear destination and the team doesn't use this to evaluate and select solutions: • Your team will not be aligned and will find decision making difficult. • Those affected by implementation won't know why the change is needed or what you want to achieve. It will be hard to engage others and feedback may be quite random and unfocused. • The credibility of your project will be low as you won't be able to demonstrate that you have objectively considered other potential options. • The team won't be able to objectively evaluate the benefit the solution delivers. Always look for ways to apply the principles as fully as you can. Time spent in confirming the destination, engaging everyone around it and gathering data to provide the basis for decisions really does pay dividends later.
There isn't any data for the process I'm looking at.	This is a common problem as many processes in difficulty haven't been looked at in this way before. Having a measurable goal at the start of the project is critical for understanding the problem and aligning the team, so getting data is one of the vital few things that you need to do. Our top tip is to use 'less is more' and only seek out sufficient data to help you understand the problem. A sample of data is often sufficient – it doesn't need to be perfect, just good enough. One team tracked a set of problems through email records to collect their data, another trawled through their calendars to collect data on time spent in review meetings. A variation on this problem is that there is *too much* data – especially on processes that are managed through an IT system. Use what matters to your customer and go back to 'less is more' – identify the data that will really help you focus.

I'm having difficulty getting to meet my sponsor.	If you are having difficulty meeting with your sponsor at the beginning of the project, put yourself in their situation. A senior manager's day is often crammed full of meetings; why should they make time for you? To get on their calendar, make sure that you have concisely articulated what matters to the customer and defined a measurable goal. Speak in positive terms about how you can work together to achieve shared goals. You may need to use a trusted intermediary (perhaps your line manager or their manager) to help you engage effectively.
	If you have done this and your sponsor is still not interested enough to make time for you, then you have either the wrong sponsor or the wrong problem – don't waste your time pushing at a closed door. Re-evaluate what you want to do, make sure your goal is aligned to company strategy, modify as necessary, and try again.
	Once you've successfully gained your sponsor's attention, be respectful of their time and clear what it is that you want from them. The sponsor contract is helpful to make your request real. Ensure that you gain their agreement to meet again at the key points.
	Further along in the project, difficulties in meeting your sponsor will often be down to scheduling issues – minimise this by scheduling all your meetings in advance after the first one. Engaging positively with the person who manages the sponsor's calendar can help with this.
The process that I'm investigating is complicated, there is no way that I can distil it into six steps.	The key is to 'start at the end' and use 'less is more'.
	The reason for documenting the current process is to gain alignment among the team members on how the process is being conducted and the issues being experienced. This is a critical input for the root cause analysis. Getting into a lot of detail is unnecessary and will be a distraction.
	When you describe the process, keep it high level and focus on identifying the *key* steps/deliverables, even if there is variation about how these are achieved. You can then document the variability as one of the issues to feed into the analysis. If there is a high degree of variation, this provides an important clue as to why the process is experiencing problems. If it is difficult for you to document, it most surely will be difficult for anyone to follow. Don't worry about comprehensively itemising all of the different variations and steps; simply record the issue to feed into the Kick-off & Analyse meeting.

A team member doesn't want to complete the team members' contract.	The team members' contract is just a way to 'make it real' and ensure that people know what they are committing to, so reluctance to complete it indicates a reluctance to commit to the project. You are reliant on your team to be successful, so address this. The first step is 'seek to understand' – ask the team member what it would take for them to commit. You will then be able to act accordingly. Often, the team member's concerns are about their day job, and if this is the case, you may need to engage your sponsor and/or their line manager to remove this obstacle. If you have taken steps to address their concerns and they are still unwilling to commit, you probably don't have the right team member, so look to replace them with someone who has the right knowledge, skills *and* attitude.
My team members say that they know what the solution is and they don't see the point in going through the Analysis phase.	This is extremely common. In fact, it is sometimes the sponsor who claims from the start that the solution is obvious. Interestingly, the so-called 'obvious' solution is often some shiny new bit of technology, expensive new system or upgrade. Explain that **to be sure** the solution will be effective, you first need to do the root cause analysis. Reassure them that the analysis phase will be short (one week). Excite them with the possibility that after you have done the root cause analysis, you may be able to find a simpler, quicker, cheaper solution. Explain that you are following a tried and trusted methodology that will 'use evidence to make decisions' and ensure that the improvement will prioritise to 'do what matters to the customer'. If the outcome of the analysis does in fact suggest that new technology is required, they will then have great data to back up the business case to support this.
My team members don't agree.	This is common in project work, and consequently, our methodology has a number of key steps directly aimed at achieving alignment. It is important to pay attention to these. Lack of alignment can delay if not completely derail the project, so don't underestimate the importance of these steps. As a team, *work **together*** to do the following: • Define the current process. The main purpose of this exercise is for the team to reach a *common* understanding of the current process and issues. • Conduct the root cause analysis – everyone has their own pet theory, and it is only by performing the analysis *together* that the team can come to an agreed conclusion. • Define the ideal process – once everyone is aligned on what good looks like, it will be easy to get alignment on how to improve.

[continued]	Often, the source of disagreement is lack of awareness of another person's perspective. This is when using the approach of 'seek to understand' can really transform a conversation, with the use of good listening techniques and paraphrasing. Equally, when team members can see that you're using evidence to make decisions, although they may be sad to drop their favourite proposal, they will be able to follow the logic which leds to that decision.
One team member is being really negative.	Use 'seek to understand' and give them a really good listening to! Often when someone seems to be behaving in a negative way, it is simply because they feel they are being ignored. It may well be that they have valid concerns. Use paraphrasing to repeat what you have heard and check it is correct. Then work together to agree the best way forward. Make sure the person concerned does at least some of the actions to bring the situation back on track.
I am feeling overwhelmed – there is so much to do.	Give yourself **less** time – what could you do in one hour? Work expands to fill the time available; for really important/difficult things, use 'less is more' and experience for yourself the power of time boxing. You are likely to be amazed at what you can achieve when you give yourself permission to fully focus on one thing for a short period of time.
We keep making the same mistakes.	Review progress regularly and conduct an AAR at the end of every meeting to 'learn by doing'. At the end of the review, make sure you agree a few actions based on your learnings to embed improvement into your way of working. By repeatedly documenting what you've learnt and taking action based on your learnings, you will see a steady improvement in capability and momentum.
Meetings have become so depressing – we just seem to spend all our time on issues.	By encouraging your team members to bring issues forward, you run the risk that the review meeting will focus exclusively on problems. There are several simple things you can do, applying the 'power of the positive', which will make project meetings engaging, worthwhile, even fun. • Start on a high – at the beginning of the meeting, make sure you really recognise and celebrate achievements and successes, no matter how small. This is critical to team morale. • Comment on how well the team is working *together* to solve problems, with reference to specific instances. • *Regularly* thank people for all their hard work – not just at the end of the project. This sends out an important message that you a) have noticed people are working hard and b) appreciated it. No one outside the team will ever really understand or appreciate everything you've all done, but you can make sure all those mini successes get a little fanfare.

The team members are raising issues which aren't even related to our project.	When your team members get comfortable, you might get more issues than you bargained for. This is where having a clearly defined destination pays dividends. Keep repeating the mantra: *'How might this issue affect our progress towards the goal?'* This will help you avoid the death knell of 'scope creep' and keep your team focused on the vital few things that will make a difference. The trick here is to make sure that the team remains focused on what matters. If issues don't affect the goal, take the conscious decision not to spend time on them. If you do this repeatedly, your team members will follow suit and ask the same question of themselves before you have a chance. Another useful approach is to take an issue offline and set up a separate meeting with the relevant people to address that specific issue.

If your particular problem isn't listed here, don't worry. Think through the three principles of success – Destination, Engagement and Iteration – together with their underlying concepts, and you will find a way to move forward.

Reading List

Title	Author	Why we recommend it
How to Run a Great Workshop: The complete guide to designing and running brilliant workshops and meetings	Nikki Highmore Sims	Includes lots of useful ways to make your meetings more engaging.
Zapp! The lightning of empowerment	William C Byham	A light-hearted book about how to (and how not to) engage your team together with practical steps you can take.
Understanding Variation: The key to managing chaos	Donald J Wheeler	A practical text which explores how to understand, chart and manage process performance.
The Goal	Eliyahu M Goldratt	A business book in novel format that explores many of the principles and concepts of the Success Equation from a different perspective.
The Visual Display of Quantitative Information	Edward Tufte	A classic book on how to (and how not to) display data to reveal its meaning.
Fast Cycle Change in Knowledge-Based Organizations: Building fundamental capability for implementing strategic transformation	Ian Hau and Ford Calhoun	Definitive paper on rapid iteration: what this means, how to do it and the benefits. Our improvement cycle is based on our experience of implementing this approach.
Sustaining Change: Leadership that works	Deborah Rowland and Malcolm Higgs	Based on solid research this provides deep insights into effective leadership and approaches to change.
Out of the Crisis	W. Edwards Deming	The inspiration and guiding light throughout our careers.

Acknowledgements

We would like to thank those who helped make this book into a reality.

Ian Hau for being our guiding light and inspiration, and Jane Seddon who challenged us to reflect and keep on learning.

Our many colleagues, team members and clients, from whom we have learnt so many things in so many ways.

Lucy McCarraher, Joe Gregory, Kate Latham and all of the team at Rethink Press; and Liz Porter at Graphics Garden for their expert support and guidance through a process that was new to us.

Our book reviewers – Emily Whittaker, Stan Kingsbury, Dave Carter and Kal Lambert – whose feedback helped us shape the book to make it more relevant and accessible to our readers.

And crucially, our families. They have patiently supported us throughout the creative process and have been a constant reminder of what is truly important.

Success Cycle Overview

Phases	Align	Analyse & Design	Implement	Run & Learn
Duration	< 6 weeks	4 weeks	6 weeks	12 weeks
Milestones	Draft Success Report	Implementation Details	Change Implemented	Final Success Report
Outputs	Draft Success Report / Team Contracts	Redesigned Process / Measures / Action Plan	Completed Actions / Process Launch	Final Success Report with Results & Learnings
Meetings	Informal meetings to develop Draft Success Report	Kick-Off & Analyse / Design / Integration	Team meet weekly to manage actions in implementation	Team meet weekly to review data & learn / Close-out meeting
Sponsor Actions	Approve Draft Success Report	Attend Kick-Off meeting / Review implementation plan	Remove obstacles	Approve Final Success Report / Celebrate with team / Publicise success & learnings

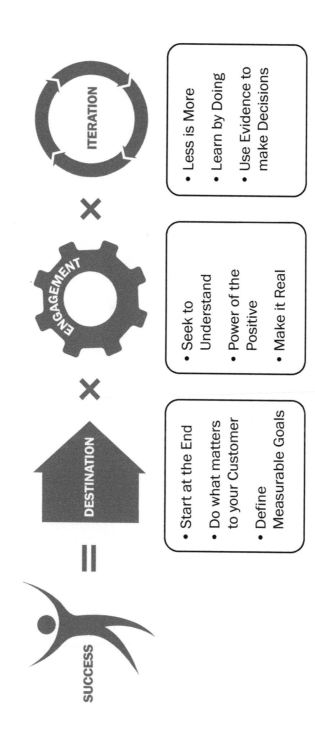

The Success Equation

SUCCESS = **DESTINATION** × **ENGAGEMENT** × **ITERATION**

DESTINATION
- Start at the End
- Do what matters to your Customer
- Define Measurable Goals

ENGAGEMENT
- Seek to Understand
- Power of the Positive
- Make it Real

ITERATION
- Less is More
- Learn by Doing
- Use Evidence to make Decisions

About The Authors

Karen Carter

Karen's real love and expertise lies in sharing simple techniques to help individuals and teams transform how they work and surpass their goals.

Karen's first experience of delivering significant improvement in business performance was in the reporting of clinical trials, where she coached teams in the reduction of reporting time from an average of 27 weeks, down to 3 weeks and ultimately 3 days. Excited by this world of possibility, Karen went on to coach teams right across GlaxoSmithKline for over 25 years. Karen has coached everyone from those just starting out in their careers to senior executives.

A consistent theme in Karen's work has been that changes must deliver meaningful benefits. For example, Karen led a global multi-million-pound savings initiative, which was successfully achieved through the delivery of over 100 individual projects.

Building on this foundation of success, Karen has also designed and led global programmes resulting in long-term cultural change, achieved through improved leadership and working practices. Programmes have been largely centred around interactive workshops where the emphasis is to 'learn by doing' and having fun!

Karen's academic studies resulted in a B.Sc. in Maths and Psychology, followed by a Masters in Biometry. This fuelled a lifelong fascination with the potent impact of combining diverse approaches. In business, Karen has repeatedly found that instilling effective leadership and teamworking habits, in combination with robust analytical approaches, enables teams to become much more than the sum of their parts.

As a Director of Delta Consulting Ltd Karen now works as an independent consultant, to support individuals and teams to achieve their business goals and enhance their capability to lead and manage change. At Delta, the aim is to 'Make a Difference'; an aspiration Karen constantly strives towards!

Marilyn Love

Marilyn's passion is delivering major business improvements by bringing focus and clarity to complex situations.

Her approach includes training and coaching cross-functional business teams and delivering the critical activities required to achieve the desired results. To do this she combines elements of process improvement, change management and project management to streamline business processes, alongside teaching her clients the skills required to independently deliver change within their teams.

As a young engineer with a Masters in Engineering, Marilyn first learnt the mantra 'Is there a better way of doing this?' and so began her career finding technical solutions to complex manufacturing issues. A thirst for continuous, practical learning led to an MBA and a Black Belt in the collaborative team methodology *Lean Six Sigma*, and instilled in Marilyn a lifelong belief in learning by doing.

Over time her problem-solving and team-leading capabilities have been applied global systems and business processes. Working in many different countries and cultures, Marilyn learnt the true value of involving staff on all levels to problem solve as teams. During a 20-year career in the pharmaceutical industry, she contributed to many business transformations in Supply Chain, Manufacturing, IT and Finance, resulting in major improvements to operations and business processes.

Since 2013 Marilyn has been an independent consultant and director with *Maywood PM*, helping companies, large and small, to kick start improvement initiatives, coaching project leaders and facilitating projects and programmes. Her approach ensures her clients have the skills required to continue sustaining the improvements and grow their capabilities over the long term.

Fiona Wilkinson

When asked what she does, Fiona's first response is often 'I help people work out how to work better'. She has helped individuals and teams to meet their business goals over decades and in many different and diverse areas: patents, pharmacokinetics, programming and pensions to name just a few. Each have delivered quantifiable benefits, some numbering many millions of pounds.

Of her many professional achievements, Fiona's personal highlights are where she has enabled others to achieve their best, or has improved the working lives of those affected by a change. For example, she maintained the focus and leadership of a key initiative through many changes of senior sponsorship, and led a radical change to the emails of over a hundred thousand people, keeping everyone working with minimal disruption as well as meeting the organisation's legal goals. She values helping charities and small organisations just as much as blue chip companies.

Whatever the challenge, Fiona achieves results through seeking out other's perspectives and forging them into a united approach to moving forward. She is known for her focus on the practical and can often be heard saying, 'How can we make that work?' She also delights in finding fun ways to help people understand new ideas, especially where they cross disciplines.

Fiona first discovered the power of combining different skills and knowledge as a biosciences specialist working on project teams. A career change to be part of a business improvement group gave her more wide-ranging opportunities to refine her abilities to lead, coach and mentor. She is currently director of Russet Consulting and enjoys helping teams and individuals work out where they need to go and how best to get there through applying the inclusive, pragmatic and simple approaches that she knows will be successful.

Contact the authors at

info@successequation.co.uk

www.successequation.co.uk

Lightning Source UK Ltd.
Milton Keynes UK
UKHW050903051119
352928UK00001B/10/P